Criminal Justice in the United States, 1789–1939

This book chronicles the development of criminal law in the United States, from the beginning of the constitutional era (1789) through the rise of the New Deal order (1939). Elizabeth Dale discusses the changes in criminal law during that period, tracing shifts in policing, law, the courts, and punishment. She also analyzes the role that popular justice – lynch mobs, vigilance committees, law-and-order societies, and community shunning – played in the development of America's criminal justice system. This book explores the relation between changes in that system and its constitutional order.

Elizabeth Dale currently teaches history and law at the University of Florida. Her research focuses on expressions of popular sovereignty, specifically popular efforts to determine and enforce notions of right and wrong, in constitutional orders. She has written several books, including the forthcoming *The Chicago Trunk Murder: Law and Justice at the Turn of the Century*. Her articles have been published in *Law and History Review, American Historical Review*, and *Northern Illinois Law Review*.

New Histories of American Law

Series Editors

Michael Grossberg, *Indiana University*
Christopher L. Tomlins, *University of California-Irvine*

New Histories of American Law is a series of bold, synthetic, and concise interpretive books that will cover all the key topics in American legal history, written by leading scholars in the field and intended for student use in colleges and law schools.

Other Books in the Series

Criminal Justice in the United States, 1789–1939

ELIZABETH DALE

University of Florida

CAMBRIDGE
UNIVERSITY PRESS

CAMBRIDGE UNIVERSITY PRESS
Cambridge, New York, Melbourne, Madrid, Cape Town,
Singapore, São Paulo, Delhi, Tokyo, Mexico City

Cambridge University Press
32 Avenue of the Americas, New York, NY 10013-2473, USA

www.cambridge.org
Information on this title: www.cambridge.org/9781107401365

First published 2011

Printed in the United States of America

A catalog record for this publication is available from the British Library.

Library of Congress Cataloging in Publication data
Dale, Elizabeth.
Criminal justice in the United States, 1789–1939 / Elizabeth Dale.
p.   cm. – (New histories of American law)
Includes bibliographical references and index.
ISBN 978-1-107-40136-5 (pbk.) – ISBN 978-1-107-00884-7 (hbk.)
1. Criminal justice, Administration of – United States – History.
I. Title. II. Series.
HV9950.D35   2011
364.97309′034–dc22   2011009932

ISBN 978-1-107-00884-7 Hardback
ISBN 978-1-107-40136-5 Paperback

CONTENTS

vii

A Government of Men, Not Laws

Histories of criminal justice in the modern West are not so much studies of substantive doctrine as studies of the rise of the State. They begin with the Weberian assumption that the modern State achieved its authority by gaining a monopoly on the legitimate use of force and trace the development of those institutions of criminal justice – police, courts, and prisons – that the State used to maintain the order that Weber asserted an advanced capitalist economy required. But there are problems with that approach when applied to the United States. As many historians have demonstrated, it cannot engage the constitutional tension between state and federal power. Just as telling, it has no room for the claims of popular constitutionalism and popular sovereignty that echoed across the first century and a half of the constitutional era in the United States.

To avoid that problem the analysis that follows takes an alternative approach, which looks at the history of criminal justice between 1789 and 1939 from a different, less court centered point of view. Its perspective is suggested by Charles Tilly's insight that "[b]anditry, piracy, gangland rivalry, policing and war making all belong on the same continuum."[1] While Tilly's focus was on the degree to which the State could act like an extralegal, even criminal, enterprise, others have pushed his idea in the opposite direction, investigating extralegal actions that entailed activities normally associated with the State. Studies of pirates and bandits, for example, have explored the ways in which groups living outside the law established their own processes of judgment and punishment. Students of civil society in the nineteenth-century United States have considered how popular constitutionalism allowed people, even those denied full citizenship, to exercise sovereign powers parallel to, and sometimes in competition with, those of the State. Other scholars have examined ways in which some private groups exercised a type of sovereign power that complemented and reinforced the institutions of the State.

To that end, this study looks at the intersection of formal law, private processes, and popular justice, exploring how and why their interplay over those 150 years prevented the creation of a Weberian State, at either the national or the local level. It considers how the constitutional order empowered popular justice, often at the expense of the rule of law, and why it tried to check its power. And it analyzes how and why that dynamic led to the shifts in constitutional theory that brought the older system to a close, and what began to develop in its place as the 1930s came to an end. To explore those issues, this book is organized in a roughly chronological fashion. The initial chapter studies the ambiguous role the national government played in criminal law from the ratification of the Constitution to the eve of the Civil War. The second chapter then moves

---

[1] Charles Tilly, "War Making and State Making as Organized Crime," in Peter B. Evans, Dietrich Rueschemeyer, and Theda Skocpol, eds., *Bringing the State Back In* (1985), 169, 170.

the discussion of crime and punishment back to the states, looking at criminal justice at the local level from 1789 to 1839. When that period began, criminal justice in the different states was decentralized, rested on local community norms, and was under significant popular control. Over the course of the next forty years, as state governments tried to Americanize the law, they attempted to make their criminal justice systems more formal and to wrest power away from local officials and communities. Those changes continued between 1840 and the end of the Civil War, and the third chapter explores the implications of that shift. By 1865 many institutional changes were in place. Police forces had been established, prison systems had been reformed, rules of procedure were elaborated, statutes modernizing criminal law had been passed, appellate opinions were published and disseminated (to further standardize the law), and lawyers and judges had begun to take control of the courts. The result was a criminal justice system that was somewhat less responsive to community norms. But popular forces of justice gained ground even as criminal justice in the courts became more formal and subject to centralized control. People in communities expressed their notions of right and wrong outside the courts, through extralegal processes of shaming, shunning, mobbing, vigilante justice, and other forms of destructive and deadly violence. In contrast to the earlier era (1789–1839), when popular forces were part of the criminal justice system, the years between 1840 and 1865 were a period of parallel processes. The State worked through the courts to judge and punish; the sovereign people used extralegal methods to take the law into their own hands.

The fourth chapter covers the period from 1865 to 1900. In the aftermath of the Civil War, efforts to wrest the power to judge and punish from popular forces were renewed. State governments (and more sporadically the federal government) expanded police forces, prosecuted extralegal acts, and used other means to try to discourage popular expressions of justice. But battles between the state and federal government checked those efforts to increase the State's power over criminal justice, and the forces of popular power continued to play a significant role in judging and punishing individuals. The next chapter then traces the effect of that intersection between state, federal, and popular forces on criminal justice in the period 1900–1936. The beginning of the twentieth century saw a continuation of efforts to increase the State's control over criminal justice at both the state and national levels. Early in the twentieth century, the creation of juvenile courts and reforms of police and misdemeanor courts were intended to give the State power over the so-called dangerous classes. In the first decades of the century, calls to end popular (or rough) justice increased as scholars, officials, and elites in both the North and South pushed to give courts monopoly control of a criminal justice system grounded in the rule of law. In some respects, these efforts were successful; efforts to end lynching largely brought that deadly practice to an end by 1936. But other types of popular justice continued to challenge the rule of law, suggesting that extralegal justice was a fundamental part of the constitutional order. So long as the targets of extralegal justice had been outsiders, the popular aspect of constitutionalism was something the constitutional order could accept. But extralegal violence seemed to spin out of control in the 1930s, affecting people and property around the country, and that prompted a constitutional shift. To explore that shift, the sixth, and last, chapter, which covers the years from 1937 to 1939, returns the book's focus to the national government. The end of the 1930s saw the beginning of a new, national paradigm for criminal justice that combined an emphasis on legality and a different approach to rights. The former used federal law to force many forms of popular protest and action out of the streets and into the courts; the latter suggested a new willingness to use the Bill of Rights to regulate criminal justice in the courts. Taken together, these changes did much to minimize the problems of the older system of criminal justice and the forces of popular sovereignty. The new constitutional order settled some problems of sovereignty, subordinating state to federal power, but the rise of rights gave people another way to check the power of the government, limiting its power.

The result is a study that traces several trends across the 150 years from 1789 to 1939. It looks at how attitudes toward popular sovereignty changed over time, and how and why claims based on rights came to supplant the notion that the people's primary constitutional role was as sovereign. It examines the way the federal role in criminal justice increased over time and sketches the impact that had on the power of the states. It considers changes within the different states and how those changes altered the role of the people in the systems of criminal justice. And it looks at how much the institutions of criminal justice changed over time and the degree to which they remained the same. Ultimately, the picture that emerges from this study is that of a criminal justice system that was far more a government of men than one of laws in the first 150 years after ratification of the Constitution. And it tries to suggest why that system had to break down. But while the interpretation put forward in this book is an alternative to the older, Weberian theory that ties criminal justice to the rise of the capitalist economy and the State, it resembles that older model to the extent that it, too, describes the connection between criminal law and constitutional order.

I

CRIMINAL JUSTICE AND THE NATION, 1789–1860

Histories of criminal justice in the West are typically accounts of the rise of the State, specifically the nation-state. Those studies trace the way central governments consolidated control over the institutions of criminal justice, a process that allowed legal processes to be standardized, helped guarantee the rule of law and fundamental fairness, and ensured social stability and order. More to the point, because "the criminal justice process [was] the most explicit coercive apparatus of the state," that process gave the nation-state the monopoly on violence that modern theories of sovereignty assume.[1]

The United States is the exception that proves that rule. Across the nineteenth century, while other Western nation-states centralized their control over criminal justice, the United States did not. Although there is general agreement on that point, there is no consensus about why the United

---

[1] Doreen J. McBarnet, *Conviction Law: The State and the Constitution of Justice* (1981), 8, quoted in Bruce Smith, "English Criminal Justice Administration, 1650–1850," *Law & History Review* 25 (2007): 593, 601.

States resisted the Western trend. According to some, it was a product of constitutional imperative: the U.S. Constitution reserved police powers – the authority to protect and regulate the health, safety, and welfare of the people – for the governments of the various states; since criminal justice fell squarely within the scope of the police power, constitutional theory required congressional inaction. According to others, it was a matter of choice: the U.S. government did not become involved in criminal law between the implementation of the U.S. Constitution and the beginning of the Civil War, because Congress refused to take much action in the realm of criminal justice and the U.S. Supreme Court held that without congressional action there was no national criminal law. As I suggest later, the evidence tends to support the latter interpretation more than the former. But to some degree, it is a distinction without a difference. For whatever reason, through the eve of the Civil War, criminal justice in the United States was not controlled by the central government and the federal government had no credible claim to have a monopoly on violence.

CONGRESSIONAL INACTION

Although Congress displayed little interest in developing an extensive system of criminal law between the start of the constitutional era and the eve of the Civil War, nothing in the text of the U.S. Constitution compelled that result or barred the creation of a national code of criminal law. On the contrary, Article III, Section 2 of the Constitution explicitly stated that the federal courts could have jurisdiction over all cases of law and equity, which seemed to include criminal law. That section also provided that all criminal cases (except cases of impeachment) should be tried before a jury. Read together, these provisions suggested that federal courts could hear criminal cases. Nor was anything in

Article I, which outlined the powers of Congress, clearly inconsistent with that expansive reading of federal power. That article gave Congress the power to legislate in the area of specific criminal laws, notably counterfeiting and piracy on the high seas. At the same time, other parts of Article I, among them its directive that Congress pass no ex post facto laws and its restrictions on the power to suspend habeas corpus, appeared to recognize that Congress could and would pass laws related to other types of crimes and punishments. And the provisions in the first ten amendments to the Constitution that related specifically to arrest, prosecution, and punishment for crimes revealed a desire to constrain the power of the U.S. government in the realm of criminal law, which seemed to imply the expectation that the federal government would act in that field.

But while the Constitution seemed to permit Congress to pass criminal laws, by and large that was an opportunity that Congress refused to seize between 1789 and 1860. During that period, Congress did pass laws prohibiting a few crimes and established an equally modest criminal justice system to enforce those laws. When it passed the Judiciary Act of 1789, the first Congress established the Supreme Court and created the lower federal courts.[2] Section 9 of that Act gave the lower federal courts jurisdiction to hear "all crimes and offences that shall be cognizable under the authority of the United States, committed within their respective districts, or upon the high seas; where no other punishment than whipping, not exceeding thirty stripes, a fine not exceeding one hundred dollars, or a term of imprisonment not exceeding six months, is to be inflicted." Other sections of the Act listed offenses punishable by death and established procedures and standards

---

[2] 1 Stat. 73 (1789).

for issuing warrants or setting bail. But although those provisions made it clear that the federal courts had some jurisdiction over criminal law, nothing in the Judiciary Act of 1789 gave any indication of what the crimes and offenses that were "cognizable under the authority of the United States" were. Did the federal courts have the power to hear cases involving common law crimes, or were those courts restricted to hearing cases on crimes that Congress identified by statute? The Act of 1789 did not say.

In two respects, the Judiciary Act of 1789 did create new mechanisms that clearly involved the federal courts and agencies in criminal justice. The Act gave the U.S. Supreme Court the right to review state court cases, including criminal law cases, which turned on questions of federal law or constitutional claims. In addition, the Act created the office of U.S. marshal, assigning one marshal to each district court. Those officials were given the power to arrest and detain, and were also allowed to employ deputy marshals as needed. The marshals and their deputies could also expand their ranks temporarily by compelling local citizens to serve as part of the *posse comitatus* when necessary to keep the peace. In addition, the Judiciary Act of 1789 allowed U.S. marshals to ask the president to call up the militia, a power that one marshal promptly used in 1792 during the Whiskey Rebellion in Pennsylvania. In other respects, in the first decades of the nineteenth century Congress was unwilling to create many institutions of criminal justice. It established courts, including criminal courts, in federal territories and also set out the laws that established systems of judgment and punishment for members of the armed services.[3] It also passed laws creating courts, including a criminal

---

[3] See, e.g., 2 Stat. 301 (1803) (judges for Mississippi Territory); 2 Stat. 359 (1806) (courts martial and judicial procedure for Army); 3 Stat. 213 (1815) (courts for Indiana Territory); 10 Stat. 627 (1855) (courts martial and punishment for Navy).

court, for the District of Columbia and established a penitentiary to hold criminals convicted in that city.[4] But before
the Civil War it did not create any federal prisons; rather, it
passed a series of laws that directed state prisons to house
people convicted of federal crimes.[5]

In 1790 Congress passed the Federal Crimes Act, but
its scope was very narrow.[6] It declared certain actions –
treason, counterfeiting or forging of public securities,
perjury in federal courts, theft or forgery of judicial
records, bribery of federal officials, and aiding the escape
of federal prisoners – federal crimes. It also made it a crime
to try to arrest foreign ministers or to engage in murder,
manslaughter, robbery, piracy, and the receiving of stolen
property on the high seas. And it set out the proper punishments for that handful of offenses. At the same time,
the Federal Crimes Act set specific limits on the power of
the federal courts (including the U.S. Supreme Court) to
review state court criminal procedures and provided that
no appeal could be taken from a state to a federal court
unless the decision of the state court turned on a federal
claim. As a practical matter, that meant that virtually no
defendant in a state criminal trial had the right to appeal
a judgment to the Supreme Court of the United States. In
much the same way, the Judiciary Act of 1789 had also
limited the power of the federal courts to intervene in
state court proceedings. The Judiciary Act declared that
the writ of habeas corpus existed "for the purpose of an
inquiry into the course of the commitment," but its reach
did not extend to those in state custody.

---

[4] 2 Stat. 390 (1805) (District of Columbia Court); 4 Stat. 178 (1828)
(penitentiary for the District of Columbia); 5 Stat. 306 (1838) (criminal
court for the District of Columbia).

[5] 3 Stat. 646 (1821); 4 Stat. 739 (1834); 11 Stat. 2 (1856).

[6] 1 Stat. 116 (1790).

Through the end of the eighteenth century, several of the criminal laws Congress passed related to slavery. In 1793 it passed the first Fugitive Slave Act, which made it a federal crime to interfere with the capture of slaves.[7] Interestingly, this law blurred the division between state and federal jurisdiction, providing that any fugitive slave could be taken before either a federal judge or magistrate or a state or local judge. The law also provided the means by which individuals indicted for crimes in one state who escaped to another could be arrested and extradited for trial. A year later, in the Slave Trade Act of 1794, Congress declared it a federal crime, punishable by a fine of $200, to carry on a trade in slaves between the United States and any other country.[8] That preoccupation continued into the early nineteenth century. In 1803 Congress declared it a federal crime to take "any negro, mulatto, or other person of color, not being a native, or citizen, or registered seaman" into any place in the United States that prohibited that entry.[9] Then, in 1807, Congress passed an Act Prohibiting Importation of Slaves, a law outlawing all international trade in slaves effective 1808.[10]

The exception to that trend came at the end of the eighteenth century, when Congress enacted the four Alien and Sedition Acts. Those Acts outlawed certain statements that were critical of the U.S. government, regulated naturalization, and gave the president the power to order the arrest, detention, and deportation of noncitizens under certain circumstances.[11] The Alien and Sedition Acts

---

[7] 1 Stat. 302 (1793).
[8] 1 Stat. 348 (1794).
[9] 2 Stat. 205 (1803).
[10] 2 Stat. 426 (1807).
[11] 1 Stat. 566 (1798); 1 Stat. 570 (1798); 1 Stat. 577 (1798); 1 Stat. 596 (1798).

were passed in the heat of an international crisis against a backdrop of internal political disputes, and many of the prosecutions under the Acts targeted American citizens for their politics. As a result, the backlash against the laws was extreme and most were allowed to sunset by 1801, although one, the Act Respecting Alien Enemies, which permitted the deportation of citizens of countries the United States was at war with, remains good law today. The Alien and Sedition Acts did not herald a period of congressional expansion into the area of criminal law; over the next fifty years Congress acted only rarely in the realm of criminal law. At the turn of the nineteenth century, Congress passed a law outlawing counterfeiting, some years later it passed a law declaring piracy a federal crime, and shortly before the Civil War it criminalized the importing of obscene materials and then passed another law declaring fraud associated with land rights in California a federal crime.[12] But generally, acts of Congress related to criminal justice were confined to areas under exclusive federal control, like Indian Territory or the District of Columbia.[13] Although there were other attempts to pass substantive criminal laws in the decades before the Civil War, those efforts routinely failed because congressmen from the slaveholding southern states were increasingly hostile to any federal act that might provide a precedent for national laws regulating slavery. Not unexpectedly given those concerns, the last major piece of criminal legislation before the

---

[12] 2 Stat. 404 (1806) (counterfeiting); 2 Stat. 423 (1907) (counterfeiting); 9 Stat. 175 (1847) (piracy); 11 Stat. 168 (1857) (obscene materials); 11 Stat. 290 (1858) (California land fraud); 11 Stat. 381 (1859) (counterfeiting military documents).

[13] 3 Stat. 303 (1817) (crimes on Indian land); 5 Stat. 318 (1838) (outlawing dueling in District of Columbia).

Civil War was the Fugitive Slave Act of 1850. That law made the process of handling claims for fugitive slaves much more perfunctory and increased the punishment for those who aided or attempted to help fugitives escape to a fine of $1,000 and six months in jail. The Act of 1850 also increased federal jurisdiction by shifting all claims to recover fugitives to federal tribunals, to be heard by federal judges or special commissioners, and compelled compliance by declaring that any U.S. marshal or officer who refused to enforce the law was liable to a fine of $1,000. It also provided that "every good citizen of the United States" was obliged to aid a marshal engaged in arresting a fugitive slave if summoned to do so. To make those activities easier and more palatable, the Act also provided that federal agents could arrest a fugitive on the basis of nothing more than a sworn statement of ownership and guaranteed that federal officers who captured fugitive slaves would receive bonuses.

A few other federal acts passed in the first half of the nineteenth century expanded federal power over criminal justice at the margins. At the beginning of the 1830s, Congress passed a law that expanded federal habeas jurisdiction by giving federal judges the power to hear cases brought by individuals held in state or federal custody so long as their petitions were for "acts committed in pursuance of a law of the United States."[14] At the start of the next decade, Congress expanded the federal courts' habeas power further, passing a law that declared that the federal courts could hear claims brought by state or federal prisoners who were "subjects or citizens of a foreign state."[15]

---

[14] 4 Stat. 632 (1833).
[15] 5 Stat. 538 (1842) (habeas for foreigners).

THE SUPREME COURT AND CHECKS ON FEDERAL
CRIMINAL LAW

Congressional inaction in the realm of criminal law was reinforced by decisions of the Supreme Court that circumscribed the role of federal courts in a variety of ways. The Court took its first, and most sweeping, step in this direction in 1812 when it declared that there was no federal common law of crimes. Although a number of lower federal courts had recognized federal common law crimes in the years immediately following the ratification of the Constitution, the Supreme Court reached a different conclusion with its decision in *United States v. Hudson and Goodwin.*[16]

That case began as one of a series of cases brought by the Jefferson administration to test the scope of the federal courts' jurisdiction over criminal law. To that end the U.S. attorney in Connecticut filed several claims of seditious libel in the first years of the nineteenth century, all intended to establish, once and for all, whether federal courts had the power to hear common law criminal claims. The claim that became the *Hudson and Goodwin* case began in May 1806, when the *Connecticut Courant*, a paper published by Barzillai Hudson and George Goodwin, ran an article from the *Utica Patriot* on its front page.[17] That article, cast as a letter addressed to the patriotic citizens of the United States, charged that the Jefferson administration had conspired with Congress to secretly pass a bill authorizing the payment of $2,000,000 to Napoleon. Although the article was more than a bit unclear, it suggested that the money was a bribe designed to prompt Napoleon to encourage

---

[16] 11 U.S. 32 (1812), affirmed *United States v. Coolidge*, 14 U.S. 415 (1816).

[17] From the *Utica Patriot*, May 7, 1806, 1.

Spain to enter into a treaty with the United States. The article ended with an appeal that the true patriots let the world know that "though vicious rulers, for a while may steal your confidence, you will not subscribe to the contract of infamy." On the basis of that article, the U.S. attorney charged Hudson and Goodwin with the common law crime of seditious libel and brought them before the federal court in Connecticut. At the start of trial, the defense argued that the federal court did not have jurisdiction to hear a case involving a common law crime; when the two judges assigned to the case divided on the issue, an appeal was certified to the Supreme Court of the United States.

The Supreme Court held that nothing in the Constitution permitted the federal courts to take on jurisdiction over common law crimes and threw the case out. That ruling stood in marked contrast to the concurrent development of a federal common law of commercial transactions, which the Court formally recognized in 1842 in its decision in *Swift v. Tyson* and which remained good law until the Court reversed it in 1938.[18] Yet *Hudson and Goodwin* cannot be read as a sweeping rejection of a federal system of criminal justice, because the Court did not hold that the U.S. Constitution rested exclusive power over criminal law in the states. Instead, the Court treated the issue before it as a problem of federal court jurisdiction, ruling that the federal courts could act only where Congress explicitly gave them the power to do so. This meant that the federal courts had no jurisdiction in that particular case; it did not mean that Congress could never create a federal criminal code or otherwise nationalize criminal justice.

Other, later decisions of the Court, although not themselves criminal law cases, did more to weaken the federal

[18] *Swift v. Tyson*, 41 U.S. 1 (1842); *Erie Railroad v. Tompkins*, 308 U.S. 1 (1938).

courts' role in criminal justice. *Barron v. Baltimore* (1833) was a case in point.[19] The decision itself turned on a claim for property; Barron argued that the city of Baltimore had deprived him of the use of his wharf in violation of the Fifth Amendment to the U.S. Constitution. The Supreme Court denied his claim, asserting as it did so that none of the provisions of the Bill of Rights applied against the state governments. That ruling, which rejected a line of lower federal court decisions that had reached a different conclusion, went far beyond Barron's argument. As a practical matter, it meant that no criminal defendant in a state court could claim that his or her arrest, detention, prosecution, or punishment violated his or her rights under the Constitution and effectively guaranteed that the protections of the Bill of Rights would provide no national standard of criminal justice or procedure.

At the end of the 1830s, another Supreme Court decision appeared to set additional limits on the national power to act in the area of criminal law. The case, *New York v. Miln* (1837), was not a criminal law case; instead it turned on the constitutionality of a New York statute that required ships' captains to turn over a passenger list within twenty-four hours of arrival in port.[20] While upholding the law, the Supreme Court declared that one of the sovereign powers retained by the state governments "extended to all the objects which in the ordinary course of affairs, concerns the lives, liberties, and properties of the people, and the internal order, improvement and prosperity of the state."[21] That seemed to imply that the Constitution gave the states exclusive claim to police powers, which might suggest that they had a power to define and enforce criminal laws that

[19]   32 U.S. 243 (1833).
[20]   36 U.S. 102 (1837).
[21]   36 U.S. at 133.

was outside of any national control. But the Court in *Miln* did not go that far, and in some subsequent decisions the Court recognized that acts of Congress could trump state laws, even in the area of criminal justice and police power. Thus in *Prigg v. Pennsylvania* (1842) the Court struck down a state law granting suspected runaways, or those who aided them, due process protections during their trials. In that case, the Court held that the state law interfered with the Fugitive Slave Act, which was an area of law that the Constitution specifically ordered Congress to regulate.[22] *Prigg* and the personal liberty laws that it struck down helped inspire the Fugitive Slave Act of 1850, with its greater articulation of the powers in federal law.

ADDITIONAL CHECKS ON FEDERAL POWER

Historical discussions of why the federal government failed to act in the area of criminal law in the first half of the nineteenth century tend to focus on acts of Congress and decisions of the Supreme Court. But from the start of the constitutional era, the federal power to define crimes, and to judge or punish them, was subject to resistance. Some of this resistance was popular. In 1794, when a U.S. marshal tried to serve writs on farmers in western Pennsylvania who had refused to pay a federal excise tax, the farmers refused to heed the writs. Instead, they formed a mob that attacked the home of the federal tax collector. Half a century later, on the eve of the Civil War, when a federal marshal in Boston captured Anthony Burns, a black man accused of being a runaway slave, a mob formed and broke into the jail to try (unsuccessfully) to set Burns free. Other abolitionists refused to comply with

[22] 41 U.S 539 (1842).

commands that they serve on a posse formed to help capture other fugitives and substituted their own sense of justice for the commands of federal law when they served on federal juries. Not all popular resistance to federal law or power was violent. In the early 1830s, a convention elected by the people of South Carolina declared that a federal tariff law was unconstitutional and void within the state's boundaries. The Nullification Ordinance passed by that popular convention further declared that any state officer who tried to enforce the federal law within the state's boundaries would be removed from office and replaced, and declared that any federal officer who tried to enforce the laws within the state could be criminally tried.

Although it is often counted as an early example of states' rights, South Carolina's attempt to nullify federal law is best understood as an expression of popular sovereignty. As the Nullification Ordinance indicated, it was an act of "the people of the State of South Carolina, in convention assembled."[23] Other efforts to check federal power came at the hands of state officials. In 1798 the legislatures of Kentucky and Virginia passed resolutions denouncing the Alien and Sedition Acts as unconstitutional. Both states tried to rally other states to join them in challenging the Acts. In 1854 the Wisconsin Supreme Court tried to constrain federal power in an opinion that declared the Fugitive Slave Act unconstitutional. Four years later, that case made its way to the Supreme Court of the United States.[24] Writing for the Court, Chief Justice Taney rejected Wisconsin's argument that members of a state judiciary could determine the constitutionality of a federal law. The Court declared, to the contrary, that the

[23] William MacDonald, Selected Documents Illustrative of the History of the United States (1905), 268.
[24] *Abelman v. Booth*, 62 U. S. 506 (1858).

supremacy clause of the U.S. Constitution provided both that the Constitution was the supreme law of the land and that the federal courts, the Supreme Court in particular, had the final say in determining whether an act of Congress was constitutional.

There were other spots of resistance to federal laws, including federal criminal law. Sitting as a trial judge in 1835, Supreme Court Justice Joseph Story declared that federal juries had no power to decide the law, a practice often known as jury nullification, and insisted that any jury that tried to do so violated the due process rights of criminal defendants in the process.[25] But federal juries continued to exercise that power, especially in cases involving slavery. In 1851 Daniel Webster, the noted Supreme Court advocate, added his voice to those denouncing jurors and abolitionists who refused to follow the federal fugitive slave laws and declared that they were engaged in treason. Yet it was a confusing time, and there were plenty of others who took a different view. In *An Essay on the Trial by Jury* (1852), Lysander Spooner argued that jurors had a right to decide for themselves what the law was because the people were the ultimate sovereigns with the power to decide the law.

CONCLUSION

In the 1830s, Alexis de Tocqueville noted that "in the United States no administrative centralization existed. Scarcely a trace of hierarchy is found there. Decentralization there has been carried to a point that no European nation could bear, I think, without profound uneasiness."[26] Certainly in

---

[25] *United States v. Baptiste*, 24 F. Case 1042, 1043 (1835).
[26] Alexis de Tocqueville, *Democracy in America* (1835), Eduardo Nolla, ed., James T. Schleifer, trans. (2010), 149.

the first half of the nineteenth century, it was true that the federal government failed to establish a centralized control over criminal justice. That was in part a result of its own failure to act and in part a result of Supreme Court opinions that seemed to check its power to do so. And partly it was because of efforts to resist its power when it acted.

2

CRIME AND JUSTICE IN THE STATES, 1789–1839

Tocqueville did not stop with his observation about the lack of central power; he also argued that the individual state governments assumed that sovereign role.[1] And histories of criminal law in the United States have followed Tocqueville. They begin from the premise that in the first century and a half of the constitutional order, from the implementation of the Constitution in 1789 to the rise of New Deal jurisprudence in 1939, the United States saw the emergence of a nationwide capitalist economy in the context of separate, *local* States. And so, instead of studying the development of a single, national system of criminal justice, those histories of criminal law in the United States look at the development of parallel, local systems of criminal law.

Because criminal justice was localized, the scope of the State in the United States was smaller, encompassing only the institutions of city, county, and state governments. Many have argued that that smaller scale was the system's greatest strength, because it permitted a degree of

---

[1] De Tocqueville, *Democracy in America*, 1: 98.

popular participation unimaginable in a nation-state; the nineteenth-century American State was responsive to local ideas of justice and the concerns of the sovereign people. In this view of criminal justice in the United States, the local State maintained order by channeling disputes into the state court system, which ruled according to norms defined and applied by the people of the community. In addition to maintaining the discipline the national economy required, these local criminal courts were subject to close scrutiny by people in the community and offered opportunities for popular participation through service on juries or the election of court judges. That combination of observation and participation was such that in much of the country (the South is sometimes cast as the exception to this rule) even those excluded from voting or holding office by reason of sex, race, or poverty could still indirectly influence criminal justice. But a closer look at criminal justice between 1789 and the end of the 1830s reveals that the situation was more complex. Even at the end of that period, the state governments had not consolidated their control over crime or its punishment, though in contrast to the federal government it was not for lack of trying.

PARTIAL TRANSFORMATION OF CRIMINAL JUSTICE

When the colonial period came to an end, the American colonies had systems of criminal justice that had been adapted from Britain, although there were differences among the state systems that reflected the variety of English institutions and customs. After the Revolution, as the state governments began to define themselves and try to consolidate their power, state leaders looked to Enlightenment debates over the nature of crime and the role of punishment to modify the systems of criminal justice they inherited from Great Britain. Their efforts to Americanize the law were aided by lawyers and judges, who set out to make their roles in the legal process more powerful, and others who viewed criminal law as the best way to guarantee order and discipline. But in the first decades of the nineteenth century, those efforts to harness the criminal law to social control, like the attempts to use the criminal justice system to consolidate the power of state governments, often were only marginally successful. Other forces, some popular, some economic, thwarted the states' attempts to become the "small sovereign nations" that Tocqueville perceived.

A trial in South Carolina, in 1805, offers a preliminary glimpse of the scope of state efforts to transform the criminal justice system in the first decades after ratification of the Constitution and suggests some of the reasons those efforts remained incomplete.[2] On October 24, 1804, Elizabeth Cannon woke to find her husband, John, dead in bed beside her. Her screams woke the household; after briefly investigating, her stepson went out to alert the neighbors and some nearby members of the family. When George Cannon, John Cannon's adult nephew, arrived at the house a short while later, he found his uncle dead with a bruised neck that bore the marks of someone's fingers and a bloody lump on his head. Faced with that clear evidence of foul play, George Cannon sent word to Justice Dehay, the local magistrate. Dehay arrived at the Cannon home around dawn and quickly put out a call for the white men of the community. Once those men got to the Cannon home, Dehay swore them in as a jury and held an inquest concerning John Cannon's death. After hearing evidence from various members of the household, including several children and some of Cannon's slaves, the jury of inquest concluded that Cannon had died sometime in the night

<hr>

[2] *Report of the Trial of Joshua Nettles and Elizabeth Cannon, for the Murder of John Cannon* (1805).

of unnatural causes at the hands of persons unknown. It quickly became clear that this anodyne verdict was a polite fiction; the jury had a very strong suspicion of who was to blame for Cannon's death. No sooner had Dehay adjourned the inquest than talk in the room turned to the likely suspect, Joshua Nettles, who had been (and many suspected continued to be) Elizabeth Cannon's lover. Nettles was a local man. He had actually participated in the inquest, though he left quickly after the hearing came to an end. Advised of the neighborhood's suspicions, Dehay immediately ordered some of the men in the room to go after Nettles, take him into custody, and bring him back to the Cannon home. When they had done so, Dehay swore some of the other men in the room in as officers of the court and ordered them to execute a search warrant, which he promptly prepared, at Nettle's home. The search party went out; they returned with some bloody clothes that apparently belonged to Nettles, a woman's shift that they had found stuffed beneath Nettle's bed, and a number of compromising letters between Nettles and Elizabeth Cannon. Armed with this evidence, Dehay ordered that Elizabeth Cannon be taken into custody as well.

Those processes of justice – the initial hearings at the scene of the crime conducted by the local magistrate, the jury of inquest composed of people from the neighborhood, the swearing in of local men as a temporary police force, and the search pursuant to a warrant – were carryovers from English practice. At the same time, as Laura Edwards has demonstrated, they were the essence of local justice, the informal, popular system of criminal justice found in the first decades of the constitutional era, a popular system that set significant limits on the state governments' efforts to consolidate and centralize control over criminal justice. The subsequent trial of Joshua Nettles and Elizabeth Cannon revealed the other ways in which informal, local practices merged with, and sometimes superseded, the formal legal processes and the rules of law that state governments tried to impose. By 1805 many states had made significant headway in changing the substantive criminal law, replacing old English rules and punishments with a rational and statutory system of criminal law. Notable figures around the country, from Benjamin Rush in Pennsylvania to Edward Livingston in Louisiana, wrote urging criminal law reform.[3] They disagreed about the precise changes that were called for, but all their proposals were intended to make criminal justice more streamlined. At the same time, these calls for reform reflected the fear that a common law of crimes gave the judiciary (and the jury) too much power. In order to check judicial discretion, and, increasingly, control the influence local jurors had on law, state legislatures enacted statutes and criminal codes.

Pennsylvania led the way, enacting laws that consolidated and rationalized the different sorts of crimes; in 1794 the Pennsylvania legislature passed a statute that distinguished between first degree murder, which required premeditation or proof that the murder had been committed in the course of another felony, and second degree murder, which included all other sorts of homicide. In addition to redefining the nature of crimes, many states passed laws that shifted the emphasis of criminal justice. In the colonial period, criminal law and criminal prosecutions were often concerned with punishing immorality. But in the years after the Revolution, state governments became less concerned with fornication and adultery, and more interested in punishing crimes of property or economy, like

---

[3] Benjamin Rush, *An Inquiry into the Effect of Public Punishments on Criminals and Upon Society* (1787); Benjamin Rush, *Considerations on the Injustice and Impolicy of Punishing Murder by Death* (1793); Edward Livingston, *A System of Penal Law for the United States* (1828).

theft. Many states continued to pass pieces of morals legislation; in 1799 Pennsylvania passed a law prohibiting work
on Sunday, and in 1801 South Carolina passed its own
Sunday closing law, but prosecutions shifted dramatically.
During the Revolution, two-thirds of the crimes prosecuted in Middlesex County, Massachusetts, were morals
offenses; by 1800 more than half of the prosecutions in
that county were for theft and less than 1 percent of the
prosecutions dealt with morals offenses. The trend was not
unique to Massachusetts; in 1830 a full 71 percent of the
cases tried in Philadelphia's courts of Quarter Sessions and
Oyer and Terminer were prosecutions for larceny, as were
50.8 percent of the cases tried in New York City's courts.
Conviction rates also reflected the new interest in property
and economic crime. In South Carolina, more than half
of the indictments in that state were for assault and bat-
tery, but crimes against property were most likely to lead
to convictions.

Yet in other respects, South Carolina was an outlier
and criminal law reform came more slowly in that state
than in others. The charges against Nettles and Cannon
reflected the state's very gradual shift away from English
law. At first glance, the charges in the case suggested a significant break with the state's English past. Blackstone, in
his *Commentaries on the English Common Law*, declared
that the murder of a husband by his wife was petty treason, a crime far more serious than simple homicide. That
distinction remained on the books in England until 1828
when Parliament passed the Offense Against the Person
Act, merging petty treason with murder.[4] But in 1805
South Carolina had already abolished the distinction, with
the result that Elizabeth Cannon was simply charged as a

---

[4] William Blackstone, *Commentaries on the English Common Law* (1769),
4: 203–204; "Offense Against the Person Act," 9 George 4 ch. 31 (1828).

principal in the second degree in John Cannon's murder. In contrast, Joshua Nettles was charged with murder as a principal in the first degree. That framing of the charges revealed how much of its English legal heritage remained a part of South Carolina's law. The terms were straight out of Blackstone, who explained that a principal in the first degree was "the actor or absolute perpetrator of the crime," while the principal in the second degree did not have to be "within sight or hearing" of the crime but could be "constructively present, by keeping watch by while another committed a robbery, or by purveying the poison the principal in the first degree used in a murder."[5]

The procedures and practices during the trial also reflected an uneasy mix of older English practice and efforts to Americanize the law. As had been the custom in England, a grand jury chosen from the community indicted Nettles and Cannon, while the trial itself was conducted before a petty jury. While members of the grand jury were typically chosen from the elite men of the area, in the first decades of the nineteenth century states gradually expanded the pool of potential jurors by reducing property require-ments for service. South Carolina was one of the leaders in this regard; a law passed in 1798 allowed any male citizen of good character and reputation who paid one dollar in property taxes to serve as a juror. That standard explic-itly excluded all women and men who did not own prop-erty or have "good character," and it was read to exclude free blacks, regardless of their property ownership. But even with those not insignificant caveats, South Carolina's law still meant that a wide cross section of the white men in a community would serve as jurors at criminal trials. In another, equally significant respect, the trial followed

[5] Blackstone, *Commentaries*, 4: 35–36.

English practice. Since the eighteenth century, England had allowed criminal defendants to have lawyers represent them at trial, and South Carolina did the same, which meant that both Nettles and Cannon had attorneys. The state was represented at the trial by a public prosecutor, a relatively recent innovation. Traditionally, criminal cases had been prosecuted privately by lawyers hired by the victims of the crime, but that changed as states embraced the Enlightenment notion that crimes were offenses against the community rather than harms to individuals. By 1820 most states had public prosecutors, though some states continued to permit some offenses to be prosecuted privately, and others allowed the victims or their families to hire private attorneys to assist the public prosecutors at trial.

As that suggests, many of the law reforms adopted in the first decades of the nineteenth century reflected efforts to make the law more modern. But sometimes American courts lagged behind their English counterparts. In England, theories of evidence and proof had become complex in the eighteenth century, but those ideas had not gained significant force on the other side of the Atlantic, with the result that the evidence at the Nettles and Cannon trial was a mix of relevant material and local gossip. Cannon's children described the discovery of their father's body, the events that followed, and their relations with Elizabeth Cannon. Other witnesses testified about the reputations of the various parties to the crime, commenting on John Cannon's reputation for peacefulness, his efforts to reconcile with his unfaithful wife, and their own awareness of relations between Joshua Nettles and Elizabeth Cannon. While one of Elizabeth Cannon's young children testified after satisfying the court that she understood the difference between right and wrong, there were no slave witnesses at the trial pursuant to the rule that slaves could not testify under oath. Nor did either defendant take the stand. Ambivalence about evidence and proof also influenced the final stages of criminal trials in the first decades of the nineteenth century. In their closing arguments, defense attorneys tended to appeal to the sympathies of the jurors in their arguments about the case, building on local knowledge and common sense. In contrast, prosecutors made very legalistic arguments that increasingly emphasized the force of the evidence, particularly circumstantial evidence. The arguments at the close of the Nettles and Cannon trial were no exception to this rule. The prosecution highlighted the strength of the circumstantial evidence against Nettles and the testimony of various witnesses that Nettles admitted he wanted John Cannon dead. Prosecution arguments also suggested it was unlikely that Elizabeth Cannon would be unaware of the fact that her husband left their bed during the night or was returned to bed sometime later, dead, and concluded she was thus a knowing and willing party to the crime. The defense, to the contrary, argued that her condition – Elizabeth Cannon was pregnant – made it likely that she had been intimidated into silence by the actual wrongdoers. To counter the testimony that John Cannon was too old and peaceable to pose a threat to his wife's younger, hot-tempered lover, Nettles's attorneys played up the evidence that he had been weak with an illness at the time of the murder. All the defense attorneys repeatedly called the jurors' attention to the lack of direct evidence tying their clients to the crime.

At the close of the arguments, the trial judge, Elihu Bay, interpreted the evidence in the case, concluding that both defendants were guilty as charged. But he did not instruct the jurors on the law. That was consistent with the view that jurors were the ultimate judges of the relevant law. That view of the jury's power had been popular before the Revolution but was under attack at the turn of the nineteenth century. The assault began in civil cases; by 1830 trial judges in most states had successfully wrested control over the law for themselves and confined jurors to finding the facts in a particular case. But in criminal law, where the idea that law had to reflect popular notions of justice remained strong, the jurors' power to judge the law and the facts prevailed. In many states, judges opted to act like Judge Bay and never gave criminal juries instructions on the law. That reinforced the traditionally local aspect of criminal law, allowing jurors to carve out personalized verdicts that weighed common knowledge of the participants and the community's sense of justice more heavily than any rule of law. That apparently was what happened in the Nettles and Cannon case. Although Judge Bay strongly suggested that both of the defendants were guilty, the jury decided to split the difference. It found Elizabeth Cannon not guilty but convicted Joshua Nettles of murder. He was sentenced to death.

Joshua Nettles did not appeal his conviction. Strictly speaking, South Carolina had no court of appeals until 1836; instead the state constitution created a Constitutional Court composed of the various circuit (or trial) judges. That court could hear a legal claim at any point in a proceeding, from pre-trial to post-trial. This, too, reflected an uneasy shift away from English practice – English law did not recognize that criminal defendants had a right to appeal until 1907.[6] In the United States, appellate courts became important in nineteenth-century legal practice, as state governments saw the courts as providing a way to standardize legal rules and end local differences in law. For that reason most states did recognize a right to appeal a criminal conviction by 1860, but the practice was slow to

---

[6] 7 Edw. 7 ch. 23 (1907).

develop and was rare in the years before the Civil War. As a result most criminal cases ended with the verdict entered at the trial court, and South Carolina, like the other states, relied on the governor's pardon power to correct errors and reduce sentences. In England, the power to pardon was used to ameliorate harsh punishments and to demonstrate the power of the sovereign state. In South Carolina and other states, governors used the pardon power to correct miscarriages of justice and reduce sentences that seemed unjust. Anyone could request a pardon: judges could initiate a request, prisoners might seek a pardon or ask their attorneys to make the request on their behalf, and sometimes the community, speaking through either the jury or petitions, might seek a pardon. There were no guidelines for the granting of a pardon; governors in some states granted them freely, others only on occasion. And it helped to have support for a request; the endorsement of a pardon by the jury or a judge, or by a petition from the community, made a pardon more likely. If public support made pardons more palatable, lack of support could cause serious problems. In Newberry, South Carolina, a convicted man was pardoned by the governor as he stood on the scaffold. No sooner had the formal legal system given up its hold on him than the crowd around the gallows formed a mob, attacked, and whipped the man severely.

PRACTICES OF PUNISHMENT, 1789–1839

Not long after he was sentenced, Nettles was hanged in the courthouse square in front of a large crowd. His punishment was yet more evidence of South Carolina's uneasy transition to an Americanized system of criminal justice. In England the list of crimes punishable by death increased between 1750 and 1825. In 1765 more than 150 crimes in England had been declared capital offenses, and that number grew to 225 by 1825. During that same period, the trend in the United States was in the opposite direction; most state governments overhauled their punishment schemes in the late eighteenth and early nineteenth centuries under the influence of Enlightenment reformers like Cesar Beccaria, who believed that punishment was the key to criminal justice and emphasized the need to make the punishment proportionate to the crime. That prompted many states to reduce sharply the number of crimes that they considered capital. In 1790 Pennsylvania passed a law declaring that several felonies, among them robbery and burglary, would no longer be capital offenses. Four years later, Pennsylvania declared that only first degree murder would be a capital crime, and over the next several decades most of the other states followed suit. Once again, South Carolina was an outlier. In 1813 it had 165 capital crimes on its books, and while the number of capital crimes recognized by that state declined in the decades before the Civil War it still punished twenty-two crimes with death. South Carolina's enthusiasm for capital punishment was unusual, but its method of execution was not. Benjamin Rush and other reformers pushed to stop public executions, arguing that they corrupted the people and too easily turned into spectacles that undermined the solemnity of the moment, but public executions remained a standard practice throughout the United States in the years before the end of the 1830s.

In the realm of punishment, South Carolina was sui generis in another way. In the years after the revolutionary era, most states began to build special prisons to hold convicts. Initially, these prisons resembled dungeons; prisoners were manacled to the wall or floor of a communal cell. In 1790 Connecticut converted an abandoned copper mine into a dungeon-like prison. But that same year marked the beginning of prison reform, as Philadelphia remodeled its Walnut Street Jail and sparked a major change in imprisonment in the United States. The idea behind that new prison was twofold. First, prisoners who previously had been assigned to do public works during the day on the streets of Philadelphia would henceforth be isolated from the populace (whether to protect the public from being corrupted by the prisoners or vice versa was subject to debate). Second, inside the new jail, prisoners would be given time and solitude to contemplate their offenses and repent their crimes. To those ends, prisoners were isolated in individual cells and required to keep silent whenever they had contact with others during the day. Practice did not completely square with that stated purpose; although prisoners were removed from contact with the public on the streets, they were not completely hidden from the public gaze. For most of the first half of the nineteenth century, Pennsylvania prisons admitted visitors for a small fee, in exchange for which the visitors were allowed to watch the prisoners go about their daily lives.

Nor, unfortunately, did the separate cells and opportunity for meditation always breed the desired penitence. In 1820 a riot at the Walnut Street Jail led to several deaths, but that did not undermine Pennsylvania's enthusiasm for the general project. That decade the state opened two new prisons modeled on the Walnut Street Jail. One, in Pittsburgh, was known as Western State Penitentiary, and the other, in Philadelphia, was known as Eastern State. Western State Penitentiary was beset by administrative problems for several years, but Eastern State quickly stabilized and began to experiment with imprisonment. There, the scheme initially set up at Walnut Street was modified so that prisoners no longer mingled with one another during the day. Instead, they remained in isolation for twenty-three hours out of twenty-four, working and living in their separate cells.

At roughly the same time that Pennsylvania was refining its penitentiary model, New York was experimenting with its own. It opened Auburn Prison in 1805, and for the next two decades prison officials experimented with living arrangements there in an effort to achieve the perfect system. During the 1820s, prisoners at Auburn, who were not given any work to occupy their time, were placed in isolation that was even more extreme than that of their counterparts at Eastern State. In an effort to use loss of individual identity as a further means of punishment, Auburn officials assigned the inmates uniforms, shaved their heads, and sharply limited their access to family, friends, and lawyers. The Auburn prisoners were also required to march to and from their cells in lockstep and to remain silent at all times. The result was a disaster. After several prisoners committed suicide and several others attempted it, the prison administration concluded the system was unworkable. In 1829 it instituted a modified system of punishment, which came to be known as the Auburn Plan. Under this new scheme, prisoners worked together during the day (in contrast to the situation at Eastern State, where they worked in isolation) and then were confined to individual cells at night. That continued to be the general practice at Auburn until overcrowding at midcentury forced the prison administration to abandon the solitary cell.

Prison reformers in Pennsylvania and New York hoped that a regime of work, along with regimented lives, would teach prisoners self-discipline and self-restraint. But if reformers intended prison labor to be only one element of a holistic effort to restore inmates to virtue and industry, in the hands of prison administrators and state governments it became the purpose behind the new prisons. After administrators at Auburn claimed that their prisoners produced such a significant profit that the prison did not need to seek appropriations from the legislature, profit making became the explicit goal of penitentiaries built in Massachusetts, New Hampshire, Ohio, Kentucky, Alabama, Tennessee, Illinois, Georgia, and Missouri. While their aims were identical, the different states pursued those profits in a variety of ways and with different rates of success. Between 1800 and 1830, penitentiary administrators in Massachusetts ran the prison industry, while in nearby New Hampshire the state sold its inmates' labor to private contractors, who employed the prisoners in shoemaking, stonecutting, and blacksmith work. Inmates at the penitentiary in Alabama also produced a range of goods, including clothing, shoes, farm equipment, and furniture, but in contrast to the prisoners in New Hampshire, the inmates in Alabama were leased to a single individual who ran the prison as if it were a small manufacturing concern.

Whether it was because of a principled resistance to the profit motive or merely the result of its famously contrarian mindset, South Carolina resisted this trend and did not build a penitentiary until 1866. In the meantime, it executed defendants convicted of many offenses, housed some in its county jails, and meted out a variety of other punishments to those found guilty. Those other methods of punishment changed over time. At the beginning of the nineteenth century, defendants in the state found guilty of theft or larceny might be sentenced to be whipped, put in a pillory, or branded. Some were banished from the state. Several of those punishments became less popular over time, by the mid-1830s the South Carolina legislature had outlawed branding and use of the pillory. But even after that, governors sometimes banished people they pardoned for crimes, and men and women were sentenced to be lashed in a public spot for a variety of offenses until the 1840s, when whipping of white convicts was abolished.

SLAVES AND CRIMINAL JUSTICE

While there were regional differences, as the various states embraced reform ideas at their own pace, by and large the criminal justice systems in the North and South moved along a similar track during the first decades of the nineteenth century. Slavery created the exception to this rule as slaveholding states passed a significant body of laws designed to control, judge, and punish their unfree people.

Slavery also gave rise to a number of institutions. Policing, including government policing, existed in premodern and early modern Europe, and colonists in North American kept the traditional English forms of policing – those comprising an elected sheriff and constable, aided by a night watch composed of men from the community. Before the American Revolution, these popularly based institutions provided the extent of policing for most of the colonies; the exceptions were those colonies with slaves. There, the desire to control the slave population gave rise to the creation of additional forces. The colonial government of South Carolina was the first to establish a special slave patrol, doing so in 1693. Other slaveholding colonies followed suit over the next century. In this early manifestation, slave patrollers' power over blacks, free or enslaved, and household servants was considerable. In South Carolina, the patrol could go into the dwellings of blacks and white servants, seize contraband items, and arrest slaves, free blacks, and white servants. Toward the end of the antebellum era, some elite whites in South Carolina talked of expanding the patrols' power so that they could arrest white poachers, trespassers, and vagabonds.[7]

---

[7] Minutes of the Beach Island (S.C.) Agricultural Club, 3 December 1859, pp. 130–131. (South Caroliniana Library, University of South Carolina, Columbia).

Well before that point, fear of slaves led Charleston, South Carolina, and a number of other southern cities to create armed, semimilitary police forces. Charleston's force, which had the power to arrest blacks and whites, was established in 1783. New Orleans created its own police department, modeled on Napoleon's *gendarmerie*, in 1805. There were significant differences between the two approaches. Members of the New Orleans force were uniformed and armed from the first (although a reform in 1809 required the officers in the force to carry sabers, not muskets, as they had previously). Unique among antebellum southern cities, New Orleans had free blacks on its police force through 1830. Between 1809 and 1836, the New Orleans' police force patrolled mainly at night, although some members of the force were on reserve during the day. As a result of reforms in the late 1830s, the police in New Orleans moved away from the military model; its officers no longer wore uniforms or carried weapons. In contrast, in South Carolina the police became more military as time went on. Beginning in 1806, police officers in Charleston were salaried, wore uniforms, and carried muskets and bayonets. Until 1821 the members of that force patrolled the city streets in platoons of twenty to thirty men; in the aftermath of the Denmark Vesey uprising, Charleston's patrolmen stopped wearing uniforms. Beginning at roughly that point, some of the policemen in Charleston also began to work assigned beats rather than march as part of a platoon.

Slavery also gave rise to a special system of judgment and punishment, because control of slaves could never be just a private matter, especially in areas where slaves made up a large percentage of the population. So by the late seventeenth century, states began to create special slave codes, and in the years that followed they established special courts to enforce those laws. In the first decades of the nineteenth century, those slave codes had become elaborate affairs that created a separate legal world. They regulated everything from crimes against slaves to crimes by slaves, provided court processes, and outlined proper punishments. In some states, the special courts handled all aspects of criminal justice involving slaves; in other states minor crimes were tried by the special courts, while the most serious offenses were transferred to the criminal justice system. In South Carolina and some other states, the so-called slave codes and courts also governed criminal justice for free blacks. These codes created special punishments for slaves. Whipping was the preferred form of punishment for many crimes by slaves, since it was punitive but did not interfere with the slave's economic value as imprisonment or execution might. But it was not the only punishment. Slaves found guilty of other, minor crimes could be branded or sometimes tied standing to a post for hours. And slaves found guilty of serious crimes, especially crimes against whites, were often executed; between 1785 and 1831, Virginia executed thirty-nine slaves who had been found guilty of raping white women.

Yet even in this highly regulated area, there were limits to State power. Slave patrols could not go into white-owned land without the permission of the owner of the property, and they could be, and often were, thwarted in their efforts to enforce laws and other restrictions on slaves by owners who refused to follow the laws. And for all states that tried to set up institutions for the judgment and punishment of slaves, the first line of discipline for slaves was personal – slave owners had the right to correct their human property in a variety of ways. Slave executions posed another point of weakness, since the desire to protect their economic investments made many slave owners reluctant to turn in slaves suspected of the most serious offences. Many states tried to deal with this by establishing a system for paying owners for slaves executed for a crime, but those processes were not always effective. Some states, like Louisiana, compensated owners at rates that approximated the actual value of a slave; others, such as South Carolina, made lump sum payments that were often well below the slave's value.

POPULAR JUSTICE

The Nettles and Cannon case demonstrates how much control the people of a community exercised in a state's criminal justice system in the first decades of the nineteenth century. The men of the community served as police, charged with seizing suspects and searching homes; they acted as jurors, weighing evidence of wrongful death, sanctioning indictments, and rendering judgments of guilt and innocence. Their multiple roles in the system meant that the popular sense of what justice required was far more important than the letter of the law. The most obvious result was that verdicts in even the most serious cases were often personalized and ad hoc, reflecting common-sense balancing rather than the commands of precedent or the terms of statutes. Not everyone was happy about that. Over the first decades of the nineteenth century, many state governments tried to centralize control over criminal law and make it more standard, but those efforts were thwarted to the extent that there were no institutional alternatives to the roles played by people of any given community. So long as the people were the police and jurors, their ideas of what justice permitted and required continued to shape criminal law.

One way to control the courts was to set limits on who constituted "the people" who could participate in those court processes. Women, children, Native Americans, and blacks were fairly consistently excluded from participation

in some or all of the formal processes of law, while poor
and transient white men were sometimes barred from participation. But in the early years of the nineteenth century,
some of the excluded were able to influence the process
of judgment in local courts in a variety of ways. Slaves,
for example, were formally barred from testifying against
whites under oath in most states, but they could testify
unsworn before coroner's juries and sometimes offer
unsworn testimony at trials. In addition, slaves could
and did share their information with their owners, who
could testify in court or otherwise act on their knowledge.
Women could testify in court, and some women, typically
older married women, sometimes served as members of
special juries called to determine if a woman charged with
fornication was truly pregnant. And as the Nettles and
Cannon case made clear, children as young as ten could
testify in court so long as they were able to convince the
judge that they understood the necessity of telling the
truth. In addition, members of all those groups could and
did join the crowds at the courthouse that watched cases
and provided the background gossip and information that
on more than a few occasions influenced legal actions or
shaped verdicts and sentences.

But the people intersected with the criminal justice
system in other ways as well. The example of the Newberry
mob at the gallows demonstrated that if the formal law
would not act, the people would instead if they thought
justice required action. Sometimes the people, writ large,
did so by working outside the courts, acting extralegally
to judge and punish offenses against their community. One
way they did so was by mobbing, another practice they bor-
rowed from England. In their English manifestation, mobs
acted to defend traditional practices, customs, and rights.
An English crowd might protest a rise in the price of some
essential good, for example, or object to the enclosure of

common land. In England mobbing was a reserve power, exercised when the sovereign failed to protect the people or appeared to be about to harm them. That traditional English understanding of the mob was transformed in the American colonies during the Revolution. Revolutionists claimed that mob action was not merely a residual right that could be exercised when the government failed to act, but a right that was fundamentally held by the people because they were sovereign. Mobbing was a powerful force from the years just before the American Revolution though the ratification of the Constitution, but in the first decades of the nineteenth century it became somewhat less popular. The practice experienced a resurgence in the 1830s; from South Carolina to Massachusetts, crowds took to the streets and other places to punish or to articulate their views of what justice required. Mobs broke up meetings on subjects like anti-slavery, women's rights, or any other topic that the crowd believed threatened the social order.

Perceptions of economic injustice also prompted mob action. In 1835 journeymen carpenters in New York destroyed furniture imported from France on the ground that the goods were a threat to their livelihood; six years earlier a group of railroad workers in Maryland had torn up tracks to protest the fact they had not been paid for their work. People mobbed to assert their sense that formal institutions were acting unjustly: abolitionists broke up court hearings to try to free people accused of being runaway slaves, and prisoners rioted to protest the injustice of their treatment in penitentiaries. Mobs also attacked people and places to enforce community moral standards. In the 1820s, mobs in New York City ransacked brothels; a decade later two mobs, one in Philadelphia and another in Connecticut, destroyed buildings they associated with abolitionism and racial mixing, while a third mob in Massachusetts destroyed a convent on the theory that the nuns inside were corrupting young women. Officials typically were unable to subdue mobs; some officials were sympathetic to their aims. At the end of the 1830s, a mob in Alton, Illinois, massed on Elijah Lovejoy's publishing house, intent on destroying his printing press so that he could no longer produce abolitionist materials. When Lovejoy tried to stop them, someone in the mob shot him to death. Speaking on the matter at a meeting convened for the purpose of discussing the problem of mob violence, the attorney general of Massachusetts justified the mob's action, including Lovejoy's murder, noting that mobbing was only to be expected when people believe "that their lives are in danger ... by the instrumentality of the press, injudiciously and intemperately operating on the minds of slaves, [to] give them reason to fear the breaking out of a servile war."[8]

Mobs were not the only groups that judged or punished people outside the courts of law. In the first decades of the nineteenth century, church congregations tried, judged, and punished their members for immorality, adultery, intemperance, and fraud. Communities used gossip to shame neighbors and acquaintances for fraud, sexual misconduct, or cheating at cards. Others took the law into their own hands as individuals, in affairs of honor, in which they fought with everything from dueling pistols to fists and knives. At its most elaborate, the code *duello* required an elaborate process before a duel could take place.[9] Seconds met and agreed on the specific terms of the engagement; they might also review the claims to try to negotiate a settlement before any duel was fought. But

---

[8] Quoted in Michael Kent Curtis, *Free Speech: The People's Darling Privilege* (2000), 246.
[9] John Lyde Wilson, *The Code of Honor, or, Rules for the Government of Principals and Seconds in Dueling* (1858).

injury to honor or harm to a family member could also be avenged more quickly and crudely at a street corner or behind the courthouse. The laws on the books in most states declared that dueling was illegal, but often the criminal justice system ignored the killing. When Benjamin Perry, a newspaper editor and lawyer in upstate South Carolina, killed Turner Bynum in a duel in 1832, he was not prosecuted. Partly that was because Perry and Bynum took their quarrel across state lines, into Georgia, outside the reach of the South Carolina courts. But writing about the incident in his diary, Perry suggested that there was an additional reason for the legal system's indifference. He observed that when he returned to South Carolina after the duel, he was approached by Bynum's brother, who assured him that the family understood why he had acted as he had and believed that he was in the right.[10] On those few occasions when the law did act against duelists, jurors often were willing to excuse defendants who killed in the name of honor, acquitting them outright or giving them minimal sentences.

CONCLUSION

In the first decades after the Constitution took effect, many state governments instituted law reforms, intended to create a new, American system of criminal law that reflected the best Enlightenment theories of crime and punishment. As part of that process, many states established new systems of punishment, reducing the number of capital crimes, creating determinant sentences for different crimes so that the punishment was proportionate to the

---

[10] Benjamin Franklin Perry, Diary 1832–1868, at August 23, 1832, in Benjamin Franklin Perry Papers (Southern Historical Collection, University of North Carolina Library).

offense, and building new prisons designed to restore the virtue and self-discipline of the convicted. But throughout the period, popular influences, inside and outside of law, undermined and weakened those efforts. The community's role in the processes of the criminal justice system meant that local standards of justice could, and did, trump the new standards set out in the law. Prisoners resisted and rioted against efforts at prison reform, while the profit motive and economic pressures undermined those efforts from the opposite direction. And extralegal forces, from mobs to duelists, acted to judge and punish outside the realm of formal law. These forces of popular justice were able to thwart the state governments' efforts to transform the criminal justice system and consolidate their sovereign power in the first decades of the nineteenth century.

3

LAW VERSUS JUSTICE IN THE STATES,
1840–1865

That basic tension between formal law and popular justice continued beyond the middle of the century, though its location shifted somewhat. The efforts of state governments to wrest control of criminal justice from local hands were more successful in those years, as they increased their control over law enforcement. Their efforts to centralize and standardize the criminal law continued to be checked by jurors' willingness to substitute their own views of justice for the commands of law. In other respects extralegal forces remained powerful and were increasingly used in competition with, or as a replacement for, the formal institutions of law. At the same time, people resorted to popular justice to challenge decisions of the formal legal system that conflicted with their sense of what justice required.

EXTRALEGAL JUSTICE

The 1830s are called the decade of the mob, but the years that followed were not much different. The flash points that had led to mobbing in the 1830s – economic injury, moral condemnation, and threats to the social order and

the status quo – continued to prompt extralegal violence
from 1840 through the end of the Civil War. In the 1840s,
weavers in Philadelphia, threatened by efforts to shift the
economies of their trade, boycotted certain employers
and beat those weavers who broke ranks; striking tailors
took similar action in New York in the 1850s. Also in
the 1850s, mobs of Germans and Irish in New York City
attempted to thwart efforts to enforce temperance legislation, while temperance mobs in other parts of the country,
often led by women, attacked saloons and grog shops. In
1844 a mob in Nauvoo, Illinois, worried about the threat
to community order and morality posed by the Mormon
community in their midst, stormed a local jail, seized the
Mormon leader, Joseph Smith, and killed him. A decade
later a mob in New Hampshire attacked a Catholic church
in Manchester in order to protest the immorality posed by
its "dangerous" teachings. Throughout the period, mobs
attacked abolitionists, shouted down their meetings, and
destroyed buildings in which they met, while abolitionist
mobs continued to try to interfere with the arrests of fugitive slaves and disrupt other proceedings and institutions
they associated with slavery.

Some extralegal groups organized to defend a particular
principle, as was the case with the vigilance committees
organized to help runaway slaves and abolitionism in
Massachusetts and New York. Other groups arose more
spontaneously, lasted only briefly, and disbanded when the
object of their ire had been thwarted or popular authorities managed to discourage their actions, as was the case
with vigilance committees organized to deal with an outbreak of horse thieves or cattle rustlers. And while some
vigilante groups stepped in where they perceived that law
enforcement was absent, others, most notably the vigilance
committees in San Francisco and New Orleans in the 1850s,
seized control of local government. In the middle decades

of the nineteenth century, no region of the country had a monopoly on this type of extralegal justice. From 1840 to 1866, there were mob actions from Pennsylvania and New York to Kentucky and Wisconsin, and vigilante groups formed from Mississippi and Texas to Iowa and Indiana.

The vigilantes in San Francisco hanged people they believed were threatening their community, and vigilantes in other states were also quick to kill or injure those they opposed. But as had been the case in the first decades of the constitutional era, not all collective action in the middle of the century was violent. Around the country, communities continued to shame and shun those whose conduct offended local mores. Groups boycotted newspapers and authors whose works they found immoral or offensive, while abolitionists organized boycotts of slave-made goods in the 1840s and 1850s to try to punish slave owners economically for their unjust and immoral lifestyle. Violent or peaceable, these groups justified their actions on a variety of grounds. Some simply took the law into their own hands, without explaining why they felt they had the right to do so. Others, notably many abolitionist groups, appealed to higher law or natural law in defense of their efforts to undermine the laws that enabled slavery. A vigilante group, formed in Indiana in 1859, offered a constitutional theory when it argued that the principle of popular sovereignty included the idea that the people were justified in taking the law into their own hands when the government failed to act. Still others asserted that when they acted they were merely applying principles of common law, like the doctrine of nuisance, and that they had as much authority as the government to enforce laws they thought were being violated.

Once again, not all extralegal actions were carried out by groups. Dueling continued, even though community leaders increasingly spoke out against the practice; most states had laws on their books providing that those found guilty of dueling could not hold public office, and states made greater efforts to prosecute duelists. But newspapers and diaries from the era demonstrate that young men from Philadelphia to California continued to fight duels in the 1840s, 1850s, and into the 1860s, and many juries continued to find duelists who were brought to trial not guilty. The 1840s saw the beginning of another way for individuals to take the law into their own hands, as husbands, fathers, and brothers claimed the right to kill men who had seduced their wives, daughters, or sisters. In 1843 Singleton Mercer of Philadelphia stalked and then shot the man who had raped Mercer's sister; at his subsequent trial the jury found him not guilty. Fifteen years later, after William Sickles shot and killed the man who seduced his wife, his attorney declared that the verdict in the Mercer case demonstrated that jurors should recognize an "unwritten law" that excused killings in cases of seduction and rape. The jury apparently agreed that the Mercer case set a precedent; it quickly acquitted Sickles, and the doctrine of the unwritten law became a new way for an individual to justify taking the law into his (or sometimes her) own hands. Other individual acts of justice, though violent, took less deadly forms. Newspaper editors whose work offended some people often found themselves the victim of a whipping that was usually administered by a man wielding a cowhide strip. Men and boys who harassed women on city streets sometimes were attacked and beaten by outraged husbands.

Extralegal efforts to judge, punish, and articulate popular notions of right and wrong continued during the Civil War. Soldiers and officers on both sides of the conflict killed one another in duels or other affairs of honor. Riots to protest the draft wracked New York and Boston, as well as smaller cities like Charleston, Illinois, and Port

Washington, Wisconsin. At their most basic, those riots were political protests, but they were also expressions of a sense that the war and draft were unjust, a view that was inspired by a mix of hostility to the people (blacks), the cause (anti-slavery), and the effect (economic hardship and loss of income). Other Civil War era riots were prompted much more directly by claims of injustice. In April 1863, a mob of women in Richmond, Virginia, outraged by escalating bread prices, attacked bakeries in the town, seizing bread and other goods for their families. Their actions initially recalled the older English principles of moral economy but quickly escalated into a general attack on stores that seemed to gouge customers. Cincinnati saw economic riots and mob actions over jobs in 1862, as blacks and whites fought to lay claim to lucrative work on the levee. There were similar riots in Toledo, Ohio, that same year, when whites rioted to enforce limits on the hiring of black workers (who were seen as undercutting wages and threatening social order). And other riots arose to protest perceived abuses of the criminal justice system. When the federal government arrested Clement Vallindigham in 1863 after denouncing the Lincoln administration, his supporters burned down the offices of a local newspaper that had called for his arrest. When a military tribunal sentenced Vallindigham to two years in prison and a federal court refused to review the sentence, indignation meetings were held in several states as Vallindigham's supporters denounced the process they considered illegal.

POLICING

In the middle of the nineteenth century, the most significant reforms of criminal justice at the state level were intended to bring extralegal activities under control. To that end, governments formed and reformed police departments to reduce the popular role in law enforcement and expand the institutions of control. Changes occurred in the extant police forces of the South: Charleston's police force expanded in the years before the Civil War. A horse guard was added in 1826, and a detective force in 1846. By 1856 the department had created a picture gallery of known criminals and had a classification system for recording arrests and convictions. With more than a hundred men in the department at the start of the Civil War, Charleston's police force was the largest in South Carolina. But by 1860 cities across the state, from Aiken to Yorkville, had police forces of their own. And those police forces became models for cities in Georgia, Alabama, and Virginia.

Few in the South questioned the value of police squads, since they were seen as an important means of controlling the states' black populations. In contrast, people in the North often objected to the creation of police departments on the ground that they dangerously increased the power of state governments. To make the point another way, police were seen as a problem precisely because they seemed to represent a step toward creating a State. Those objections meant that efforts to establish police forces in the North were sporadic and haphazard. In 1833 Philadelphia briefly created a day watch to complement its night watch, but it had no permanent police force until the 1840s. Boston established a police department a few years earlier, in 1838, but New York City continued to rely on a combination of elected constables, appointed day marshals, and night watchmen until the 1840s. In 1836 a committee appointed by New York's mayor recommended that the city create a police force modeled on the City of London police, but the proposal was ignored. There was a second effort to create a New York City police force in 1844, when the state legislature recommended that the city create a "Day and Night Police" of five hundred men, once again using London's police as a model. The city government refused to go that far, although the mayor did appoint a uniformed police force of two hundred men. That force lasted only as long as the mayor's term; when the new Democratic administration took control of the city government the next year, it implemented the legislature's recommendation and created a force of five hundred men. In contrast to the semimilitary-style organizations favored in southern states, at first the officers in the police departments created in New York, Boston, and Philadelphia wore no uniform and carried no weapons, though officers in the New York police were given special badges. This began to change just before the Civil War. In New York, members of the police force were given uniforms in 1855 and were officially allowed to carry guns in 1857. Philadelphia's officers were given uniforms in 1860; Chicago's police officers had to wait until 1863 for theirs. At roughly the same time, these northern cities began to create hierarchical chains of command for their police departments and otherwise expand their scope. Boston created its first detective force the same year as Charleston; New York City established its detective force in 1857.

If the desire to suppress slave uprisings drove the creation of police forces in southern cities, fear of riots and mobs led to the creation of organized police forces in the north. Boston's police department was formed a few years after the riot that destroyed a Catholic girls' school; New York's efforts to establish a police department began in earnest after violent riots in 1843; Chicago set up its police force after the Lager Beer Riot in 1855. Perhaps because the creation of police departments in the North had been limited by the concern that the police might become a standing army, once established the police forces in northern cities were largely untrained. As a result, their activities created disorder as often as they restrained it. In theory, police officers in northern cities had the power to arrest anyone and were charged with handling all kinds of crimes; in practice, they tended to focus their attention on the lower classes and limited their efforts to breaking up fights and suppressing violence (especially during riots). Narrow as those duties were, the police were often attacked for being unable to perform either effectively. In fact, this was a universal problem; governments in both the North and South often had to call in the militia to help the police maintain order. And private citizens engaged in their own forms of self-help; in the decades before the Civil War, men from New Orleans to New York armed themselves for their own protection. The sword cane was the weapon of choice among elites until the revolver became a handy alternative. Men in the working class used knives and bare fists for the same purpose. On some occasions, popular frustration with the police went further, prompting revolts against the local government. The vigilance committee that took over San Francisco in 1851 claimed it did so because the city government and its police department could not keep order. In 1858 the vigilance committee formed in New Orleans made the same claim when it seized the state arsenal and police headquarters. Unable to subdue the vigilantes in his city, the mayor of New Orleans declared them special police officers. That did not resolve matters. Violent altercations followed, the mayor was impeached, but the vigilance committee did not disband until its party lost the next election.

CRIMINAL LAW AS SOCIAL CONTROL

In the years between 1840 and 1865, legislatures continued their efforts to control the people through law. The first decades of the nineteenth century had been marked by the passage of laws that punished economic or property-related crimes, and this continued after 1840. At the same

time, states also enacted laws that criminalized other types
of activities. As William Novak has demonstrated, local
governments had regulated all sorts of activities, occupa-
tions, and industries even in the colonial period, and state
and local governments continued that practice into the
first half of the nineteenth century.[1] These regulatory laws
often included criminal penalties for failure to comply with
the law. While continuing that practice, in the 1830s states
also began to try to regulate morals offenses. Statutes prohibiting adultery, fornication, incest, and sodomy were
passed in states as far apart as Maine and Michigan in
the 1830s. That same decade Illinois passed a law prohibiting the sale of playing cards, dice, billiard balls, and
obscene materials. The pattern continued over the next
several decades: temperance laws swept New England in
the 1850s, and California passed a series of Sunday closing laws in the 1850s. One California law, passed in 1855,
outlawed noisy amusements on Sunday; another, passed
in 1858, closed stores and prohibited the sale of goods.
Typically, these laws were intended to increase state control of behavior and were prompted by fears that urban-
ization was exposing people, especially young men and
women, to corrupting influences. To that end, enforcement
often targeted particular groups; in St. Louis, brothels
were winked at during the 1840s, while prostitutes who
worked the streets were arrested.

Sometimes these laws were challenged as infringements
on individual rights guaranteed in state constitutions;
while courts typically upheld the laws, they responded
to the challenges in a variety of ways. Some justified the
outcome on pragmatic grounds. In 1848 the Pennsylvania
Sunday closing law was upheld against a challenge by a

[1] William J. Novak, *The People's Welfare: Law and Regulation in
Nineteenth-Century America* (1996).

Seventh Day Baptist.[2] The court noted that Sunday had long been a day of rest and tranquility, and concluded that the law simply codified that custom. Other decisions took a much more religious approach. In 1854 the Missouri Supreme Court rejected a saloon keeper's challenge to a Sunday closing law, holding that the state and nation had been founded by Christians, who would have approved of laws that protected the opportunity for worship.[3] The court noted there was no violation of the state constitution because no one forced the saloon keeper to worship on Sunday if he chose not to do so. But while states passed Sunday closing laws, often as a result of pressure by groups that were interested in enforcing a morality based on Christian (typically Protestant) precepts, and other forms of morals legislation, and courts were willing to uphold them on a variety of grounds, by the 1860s these laws were rarely obeyed. Attempts from 1859 to 1867 to enforce a law in Philadelphia that prohibited the operation of horse cars on Sunday were unsuccessful; by 1870 a similar ban in New York was a nullity.

That sort of resistance was another example of how the people could influence the law. At the same time, the formal challenges to the Sunday closing laws based on rights, unsuccessful as they often were, reflected an important trend in the years before the Civil War. Rights became an important part of legal discourse in this period, when appeals to rights were made by a variety of groups in a number of contexts. Abolitionists used claims of rights to justify their extralegal actions; women sought, and were extended, property and economic rights by the Married Women's Property Acts that were passed by many states to protect their claims against depredations by their husbands.

[2] *Sprecht v. Pennsylvania*, 8 Pa. 312 (1848).
[3] *Missouri v. Ambs*, 20 Mo. 214 (1854).

But while appeals to rights in those instances empowered and protected, rights also justified hierarchy and privilege. Most obviously, the slave owners who attacked any law that interfered with their claims to human property framed their arguments in terms of their rights. That reflected a larger constitutional problem, the rise of a hierarchy that privileged those who could lay claim to a full range of inalienable rights over those whose rights were more limited or whose claims to rights were more easily restricted by law. The use of rights to create hierarchies of citizenship underpinned the decision in *Scott v. Sandford* (1857), the infamous *Dred Scott* case, which equated citizenship with the possession of inalienable rights.[4] While the decision formally declared only that free blacks, like slaves, could never be citizens because they lacked inalienable rights, as Justice Curtis noted in dissent, it raised serious questions about the status of white women as well.

Other attempts to challenge or reform the assumptions of the criminal law in the middle of the century were equally unsuccessful. In the late 1830s and the 1840s, doctors and other reformers pushed courts and legislatures to modify the insanity defense. The original rule of criminal intent, inherited from English law and set out in Blackstone, was that lunatics, like children, were "incapable of committing any crime, unless in such cases where they show a consciousness of doing wrong, and of course a discretion, or discernment, between good and evil."[5] This led to the idea that an insane person could not be found guilty of a crime and punished, because he or she lacked the requisite intent. But courts interpreted this to mean that a person, to be declared insane, had to be completely destitute of reason. In the

---

[4] 60 U.S. 393 (1857).
[5] Blackstone, *Commentaries*, 4: 195–196.

early nineteenth century, medical scientists on both sides
of the Atlantic tried to change that rule, to allow criminal
courts to recognize that people in the grip of a particular
passion (or mania) might be insane. In a setback for those
efforts, in 1843 the High Court of Parliament adopted
the M'Naughton rule, which turned on whether a defendant could tell right from wrong. According to that test,
a defendant could be deemed insane only if, at the time
of the crime, he was "laboring under such a defect of
reason, from disease of the mind, as not to know the
nature and quality of the act he was doing; or, if he did
know it, that he did not know he was doing what was
wrong."[6] In the United States, many courts adopted a
similar rule, though some tried to take a different path.
In *Massachusetts v. Rogers*, Chief Justice Lemuel Shaw
ruled that a person acting on an irresistible impulse could
be insane, even if he was able to articulate the distinction
between right and wrong.[7] Shaw's opinion emphasized
the question of self-control; those who were unable to
control themselves by reason of a mental defect were
insane. While Shaw was an influential jurist, his opinion
in *Rogers* did little to shift the landscape of the law in the
United States. Jurors' attitudes also posed a problem for
efforts to reform the law of insanity. In some courts and
cases, jurors who felt that the law related to insanity was
too harsh sought pardons for defendants they believed to
be insane; in other cases, jurors ignored their instructions
and held defendants guilty even when their conduct fell
within the letter of the insanity law.

There were other efforts to make the law more easily
known and followed. Continuing the process they had begun
earlier, state governments published collections of statutes

[6] *Daniel M'Naughton's Case*, 8 Eng. Rep. 718 (1843).
[7] 11 Am. Dec. 458 (Mass. 1844).

on a regular basis and the state courts established systems to publish court opinions. Treatises, typically aimed at lawyers and judges, helped this process along. In the first decades of the nineteenth century, those books on law were summaries of English practice, modestly adapted for American use. This began to change in the late 1820s. James Kent, a chancellor in New York, published his *Commentaries on American Law* in 1826, Joseph Story published his *Commentaries on the United States Constitution* in the 1830s, and Theophilus Parsons published his *Commentaries on American Law* in 1836. The first American treatise on criminal law, Francis Wharton's *Treatise on the Criminal Law of the United States*, came out in 1846. Those books organized statutes and appellate court rulings to suggest trends and establish general rules of law.

COURT REFORMS

By 1840 most states permitted appeals from criminal convictions, though Louisiana did not do so until 1843. But while the possibility of appeal existed, it was effectively a privilege because few defendants could afford it. The Wisconsin Supreme Court heard 27,000 appeals in the 120 years between 1839 and 1959; of those only 1,400 were appeals from criminal cases. In other states, appeals remained a relatively unimportant part of the criminal justice system though World War I.

Other reforms were more effective but created new tensions that set institutions of criminal justice at odds with one another. That was what happened in the petty criminal courts, especially in cities. Those courts heard minor criminal matters, and in the early decades of the nineteenth century they had been places where many minor claims were prosecuted by private parties. Few lawyers were involved, and the judges often had no formal legal training. As Allen Steinberg's study of Philadelphia demonstrated, those courts had been a readily available space in which local people could seek out justice, recourse, or revenge, where the justices and magistrates could help people negotiate and defuse neighborhood tensions.[8] Yet in the eyes of some reformers, those informal processes demonstrated that the petty courts were insufficiently legal. Far from being courts, they seemed to be places of rough justice, on a par with the dueling ground, the barroom floor, and the corner alley. Reformers targeted those courts, but it was the rise of organized police forces in the 1840s that did the most to undermine them. As arrests for minor crimes swamped the courts, judges began to spend less time trying to defuse or negotiate claims and subjected more defendants to summary punishment.

There were also problems in the felony courts. Even as those courts became more formal in their processes and more committed to the rule of law, they still gave pride of place to jurors. Coroner's jurors continued to be called in cases of sudden death and still rendered verdicts that ignored clear evidence of crimes. Grand juries weakened the rule of law by choosing not to indict a significant number of people brought before them. And the trial jury remained a significant check on the states' ability to use the courts to centralize their power. Writing in 1838, Philip Hone had complained that jurors in New York City were unwilling to convict people for murder.[9] The problem was not confined to New York. In his extended study of violent death in Philadelphia, Roger Lane found that the *murder rate* for that city rose modestly between 1839 and 1859. But he also found that in the same period the *conviction rate* for

---

[8] Allen Steinberg, *The Transformation of Criminal Justice: Philadelphia, 1800–1880* (1989).
[9] *The Diary of Philip Hone, 1828–1851* (1927), Vol. 2: 47–48.

murder declined significantly.[10] Between 1839 and 1846, 59 percent of the people indicted for murder in Philadelphia were brought to trial, and slightly less than two-thirds of those tried were found guilty. In the period between 1846 and 1852, while the percentage of people indicted for murder increased, the proportion of those who were tried and convicted for murder dropped to 58 percent. Between 1853 and 1859, the percentage of people who were indicted remained roughly the same, but the proportion of those who were tried for murder and convicted declined precipitously, to 47 percent. Studies of other places show similar results. Eric Monkkonen's study of New York City found that in the antebellum era less than a third of the men brought to trial for murder were convicted.[11] In yet another study, Jack Kenny Williams determined that jurors in antebellum South Carolina found criminal defendants guilty only 39 percent of the time. He also found that about half of the people tried for murder in South Carolina in that same period were convicted of the lesser crime of manslaughter; in 1845 Charles Price, from Edgefield, South Carolina, shot Benjamin Jones because Jones had called Price's daughter a liar.[12] A grand jury promptly indicted Price, but the jury at his trial just as quickly rejected the charge and found Price guilty only of manslaughter. An equally sympathetic judge then sentenced Price to a single year in jail.

In some states, judges responded by trying to deny criminal juries the power to decide the law, but there was considerable resistance to that effort. In the 1840s, the Massachusetts court declared that jurors in criminal cases

---

[10] Roger Lane, *Violent Death in the City* (1979), tables 8, 10–12.
[11] Eric H. Monkkonen, *Murder in New York City* (2001).
[12] Jack Kenny Williams, *Vogues in Villainy: Crime and Retribution in Ante-bellum South Carolina* (1959), 85.

could do no more than apply the law as given to them by the trial judge.[13] The state legislature then passed a law that seemed to repeal that ruling, restoring the power to decide the law to the jurors.[14] But the Massachusetts Supreme Court once again intervened, ruling in 1855 that the statute did not mean what it said and that jurors in criminal cases could judge only the facts, not the law.[15] Courts in Kentucky, Maine, and Missouri also tried to restrict the power of the jury.[16] Increasingly, the argument for this restriction rested in the new language of rights – courts argued that defendants on trial in criminal cases had a due process right to a fair trial and legal certainty, a right that was undermined by jurors who substituted their ad hoc sense of what was just for the rule of law.[17]

But as often as prosecutors or judges made that point, defense attorneys undermined it. They read the law to the jurors, and they appealed to principles of divine justice and mercy or to theories of unwritten law. The idea that jurors could and should decide the law was given constitutional credit by a number of thinkers, and in some states, the government seemed to agree. Since the 1820s, Illinois had recognized that jurors had a right to substitute their view of the law for that given to them by the judge; in the 1850s, Maryland and Indiana enshrined a similar principle in their state constitutions.[18]

---

[13] *Massachusetts v. Porter*, 51 Mass. 263 (1845).
[14] 1855 Mass. Acts c. 152.
[15] *Massachusetts v. Anthes*, 71 Mass. 185 (1855).
[16] *Montee v. Kentucky*, 26 Ky. 132 (1830); *Hardy v. Missouri*, 7 Mo. 607 (1842); *Maine v. Wright*, 53 Ma. 328 (1865).
[17] This theory was first articulated by Justice Story, sitting as a trial judge, in *United States v. Battiste*, 24 F. Case 1042, 1043 (1835).
[18] Law of Illinois (1827), §176; Maryland Constitution, Art. X, §5 (1851); Indiana Constitution, Art. 1 §19 (1851).

THE INTERSECTION OF LAW AND JUSTICE

Even though the states managed to reduce some of the popular aspects of the criminal justice system, at the middle of the nineteenth century the criminal courts remained a space in which justice and law sometimes collided and the result could be a complicated, multifaceted business, as *Kentucky v. Ward*, a case from 1854 demonstrated.[19] The case began when Matthews Ward, the oldest son of Louisville's richest man, marched into Louisville High School accompanied by two of his younger brothers, Robert and Will. The Wards went to the schoolhouse to demand an apology from the school's principal, William Butler, who had whipped Will the day before after catching him in a lie. Confronted by the three Wards in front of a classroom of students, Butler refused to apologize or retract his claim that Will had lied. After Ward and Butler exchanged heated words, Butler moved toward Ward and grabbed his arm. Ward responded by pulling a hand, bearing a pistol he had purchased just that morning, out of his pocket. He shot Butler at point blank range. And then, as Butler fell to the ground, mortally wounded, the Ward brothers left the school. That evening, the sheriff took Matt Ward and his brother Robert into custody. As they sat in the jail, a hunt for lawyers began. The Wards' father used his wealth and connections to hire most of the famous lawyers in the state, including John Crittendon, who recently had been appointed to represent Kentucky in the U.S. Senate. The Butler family, who had been leaders in education in Louisville for several generations, were able to use their connections to hire some attorneys to assist the state's attorney general in his

[19] A. D. Richardson, *A Full and Authentic Report of the Testimony in the Trial of Matt. F. Ward* (1854).

prosecution. The defense then asked for, and got, a change in venue, on the ground that emotions in Louisville were too high to allow the case to be tried in that town. Ignoring state law, which required that a case be transferred to the next nearby county, the judge shifted the case several counties over, to Elizabethtown. There, after hearing the state's evidence, which consisted mostly of the testimony of the various schoolboys who witnessed the killing, and the defense evidence, composed of testimony suggesting that Matt Ward suffered from ill health and was reasonably apprehensive of being harmed by the more robust Butler, the jury acquitted Matt Ward. The prosecution immediately dismissed the charges against Robert Ward, and the two youths walked out of the courtroom free men.

That outcome depended on the shift to a more formal, less local criminal justice system. Far away from Louisville, the trial went on without the sort of local knowledge that had marked the trial of Nettles and Cannon in South Carolina in 1805. The jurors in Elizabethtown had no personal knowledge of Matt Ward or William Butler, no way of weighing the claim that Ward was physically no match for the schoolteacher. Nor could they bring their own understanding to bear on the defense claims that Matt Ward was normally a pacific and quiet person or that the schoolboy witnesses had probably testified falsely in the case under the influence of one of their teachers. Because they lacked any personal acquaintance with Will Ward, the jurors had no way of knowing whether he had a tendency to lie. Instead of viewing the case through the lens of their prior, personal knowledge of the parties, the jurors were forced to decide the case on the facts that were admitted at trial, as shaded and sometimes shadowed by the arguments of counsel. Significantly, they received little formal assistance from the court. Notwithstanding the requirement in Kentucky that the jury apply the law as given to them by the judge, the trial judge in this case did no more than note that the various attorneys had all adequately addressed the law in their arguments.[20]

That suggests the case was nothing more than another example of jurors' willingness to excuse murder, but the verdict was not the end of the story. When word of the trial's outcome got back to Louisville, many of the people in the city were outraged. A crowd estimated at ten thousand people gathered in the courthouse square that evening to hear speeches and express their fury. Most of the crowd stayed at the courthouse, burning effigies representing the jurors, the judge, and several of the lawyers in the square, but roughly two thousand people left the courthouse and marched to the Ward mansion. There they chanted and threw rocks, breaking the windows of the house and conservatory. Then they made effigies of the two Ward brothers, lit them, and threw them at the house. Although a corner of the front entranceway caught fire, the fire went out before more damage was done. That was the end of the protest that evening in Louisville, but it was not the last protest against the verdict. Over the next several weeks, other mobs gathered to voice their disapproval in Louisville and other towns across the state. Ultimately the protests died down, and the Ward family was able to return home. Even then, however, the community stayed on the watch. Word went out that if Matt Ward, who had fled Kentucky after the verdict, tried to return to Louisville he would be stopped. Ward never did go back; he moved to a family plantation in Arkansas, where he was killed during the Civil War by a troop of southern soldiers who mistook him for a Union spy.

Excerpts from the speeches made during the protests in Louisville reveal that the mob was angered by several aspects of the case. They objected to the verdict, which they

---

[20] *Montee v. Kentucky*, 26 Ky. 132 (1830).

felt was unjust, and were outraged by the defense attorneys' attacks on the honesty of the schoolboy witnesses. Finally, they objected to the fact that the case was tried so far away. Read as a whole, the protests were both a defense of local justice and honor, and an attack on the way the legal system had denied the former and impugned the latter. Matt Ward got away, but mobs in other places were able to take actions that simultaneously condemned the legal system and punished the wrongdoer. In 1855 Adolphous Monroe was tried and convicted of murder in Illinois. He was sentenced to death, but the governor of the state pardoned him on the eve of his execution. When word reached Cole County that Monroe would not be hanged, a mob gathered and marched on the county jail. As the sheriff stood aside, the mob broke into the jail, seized Monroe, and hanged him.

CONCLUSION

A variety of changes, from the creation of police forces to the reforms of petty courts, helped transform the institutions of criminal justice between 1840 and 1865. Although those reforms did not always achieve their desired ends, they did help weaken the role the people played in the criminal justice system in the various states. Other changes also modified the legal landscape; by the 1850s, the language of law and of rights had become not just a rule of decision, but a dominant language that spilled out of the courts and into hearings before church congregations and day-to-day transactions. Yet those linguistic shifts also empowered some at the expense of others. But significant as they were, these alterations were not enough to turn the individual states into little sovereignties. Problems within the institutions of law prevented the state governments from using them to cement their sovereignty, and extralegal forces continued to act as a counterweight to state power.

4

STATES AND NATION, 1860–1900

The changes in criminal law in the first half of the nineteenth century at best were gradual and incomplete; those that followed the end of the Civil War often were quicker, but still were limited. Shifts in the country's social dynamics drove state governments to try to expand their powers, while pressure from reformers and the desire to circumvent the powers of popular justice prompted other efforts to strengthen state-level institutions of criminal justice. At the same time, the national government, which had expanded its power during the war and Reconstruction, tried to assume a greater role in criminal law. All those efforts to bring crime and criminal justice finally under government rule were countered once again by popular forces, from the rough justice of the lynch mob to the more subdued, but not less significant activities of law-and-order leagues. And those familiar attempts to maintain the sovereignty of the people were both complemented and thwarted by renewed attempts to appeal to rights. All this meant that the last decades of the nineteenth century were a period of great flux in criminal justice; yet when that century came to a close, the fundamental tension between formal law and popular justice remained.

REFORMING CRIMINAL JUSTICE IN THE STATES

In the second half of the nineteenth century, state governments expanded their efforts to use the criminal law to discipline and control their populations. Beginning in the 1870s, many states passed laws regulating obscenity; others criminalized the use of drugs or passed temperance legislation. Often, these laws reflected considerable lobbying by reform groups, some dominated by women: the dispensary laws, which regulated the sale of alcohol in South Carolina, passed in 1894 following a decade and a half of lobbying by the Women's Christian Temperance Union and local women's groups. Other efforts, only some of them successful, were made to regulate sexuality as well. In the 1860s and mid-1870s, lawmakers in New York debated legislation that would have permitted prostitution in the city, but required that all prostitutes be licensed and subject to medical examination. While that effort failed, St. Louis succeeded in passing a licensing law for prostitutes in 1870, but that law was repealed in 1874. In another, more successful campaign, doctors who sought to increase their professional authority managed to restrict the power of midwives in the second half of the century and criminalize the practice of abortion.

In the same period, the fear that the young women who flocked to the cities in search of jobs were inadequately protected against sexual predation led states to pass statutory rape laws and raise the age of consent. The fate of those laws in the last decades of the century offered an example of how laws could be subverted, demonstrating the continued weakness of the state. From Vermont to California, the reformers who pressed for statutory rape laws hoped to protect young women from older men, and in a few states, like Vermont, those aims influenced prosecution. But in California, the purpose of the law was subverted from the first. Initially, arresting officers, prosecutors, and judges undermined the law, choosing to protect men charged with statutory rape by refusing to arrest, prosecute, or convict them. After judges who were more sympathetic to the law's aim were put on the bench, efforts to enforce the law to protect young women were complicated, and not infrequently thwarted, by parents who tried to use the law to control their teenage daughters. What began as a paternalistic effort to protect vulnerable young women became a means of controlling those women instead. The problem of popular resistance to law was not confined to statutory rape or morals legislation. The Illinois Civil Rights Act, passed in 1885 to guarantee civil and criminal remedies for blacks deprived of access to public businesses because of their race, was a case in point. In 1889 the Supreme Court of Illinois affirmed the law in a widely publicized decision, but shopkeepers and other business owners routinely ignored the law and the police did little to enforce its provisions.[1]

Other efforts at reform centered around policing. During Reconstruction several southern cities, including Wilmington, North Carolina, modestly integrated their police forces by adding black officers. Other cities experienced much greater integration; by 1876 half of the officers on the police force in Charleston, South Carolina, were black. But Reconstruction's end in 1877 put a stop to that experiment, along with so many others. While there were some African American police officers on the Tampa, Florida, police force in the 1880s, in Wilmington, North Carolina, as late as 1898 and in Tulsa, Oklahoma, in 1917, those officers represented the remnants of the earlier pattern, not a well-established hiring practice. After its only

[1] *Baylies v. Curry*, 128 Ill. 287 (1889).

African American policeman retired, Tampa did not hire another black until 1922. Nor were the numbers of African American officers particularly significant on police forces in the North. Chicago hired its first black officer in 1873, but forty years later, when African Americans represented 6 percent of the city's population, they made up only 2 percent of the officers in the Chicago police department. The situation with respect to women was not even that good. Even before the Civil War, some police departments had begun to hire women to serve as matrons to handle women arrestees. But many governments resisted this reform; in the mid-1880s, a newspaper in Milwaukee, Wisconsin, denounced as ridiculous a proposal that that city hire matrons. And the idea that women might be hired as police officers or detectives had no traction; not until 1905 did a woman in the United States serve as a police officer.

Another late-nineteenth-century reform effort tried to distance the police from both the people and politics. In response to complaints that officers took bribes, displayed political or ethnic favoritism, or turned a blind eye to crime, local governments attempted to professionalize their departments. As part of that effort, many northern cities completed the shift to a hierarchical, centralized police force that they had begun before the Civil War. The process took a variety of forms. Police officers in St. Paul, Minnesota, began to wear uniforms in 1872; the officers in neighboring Minneapolis did so in 1876. In 1888 Cincinnati created a police academy to train officers; New York implemented an informal training program in the 1890s (though it did not create an actual academy until 1909). This second generation of reform had two significant consequences. The creation of a level of high-ranking police administrators and officers established a group that could and did share information across state lines, which marked the beginning of a nationwide crime control network. At the same time, professionalization of the rank and file meant the job of police officers was redefined. In the 1870s and 1880s, some police departments served as a sort of crude safety net, offering shelter to the homeless and temporarily destitute. By century's end, local police, especially in the nation's cities, were occupied almost exclusively with crime prevention and control, not social services.

Unfortunately, those reforms did little to alter the basic perception that the police were corrupt and incapable of preventing crime or apprehending criminals, nor did they put an end to political influence on police departments. Although centralization was intended to remove the police from political control , that goal was often undermined by the politicization of appointments to the central command. And reforms could not completely separate the police from popular forces. South Carolina's Ellenton Riots, in 1876, began when the local sheriff called in an all-white posse to help capture blacks he suspected of helping conceal a black rape suspect. The posse quickly became a mob, setting off a weeklong race war. A decade later, in 1888, a white mob in Forest, Illinois, helped a sheriff there capture a young black man suspected of murdering a white co-worker; the evidence suggests that the mob roughed the suspect up in the process.

Efforts to reform jurors' role in the criminal justice system were equally ambitious, and sometimes successful. Coroners, and their juries, were the targets of many reformers who wanted to make investigations of unexpected deaths more scientific. Massachusetts replaced its coroner with a medical examiner in 1877, and counties in New Jersey had medical examiners by 1901, but most jurisdictions did not follow the Massachusetts lead. New York continued to rely on a coroner until 1915, while some counties in Wisconsin retained the office until after World War II. Other attempts to reduce the power of grand juries were more successful.

The California Constitution of 1879 allowed prosecutors to bypass the grand jury in felony cases by bringing a suspect before a judicial officer for a preliminary hearing on the state's evidence. If the judge found sufficient evidence to proceed, he would issue an information and criminal proceedings would begin without recourse to the grand jury. The practice became the rule, not the exception, in California by the 1880s, and other states began to adopt the approach as the century came to an end.

Courts and legal scholars redoubled their attempts to restrict jurors in criminal cases to judging the facts, not the law. When the Supreme Court of Pennsylvania declared jurors' right to decide the law "one of the most valuable securities guaranteed" by the state constitution, the legal scholar Francis Wharton denounced the ruling.[2] Wharton argued that letting jurors decide the law based on their political or racial prejudices posed a serious threat to the liberty of criminal defendants. A second legal scholar, Decius Wade, also fought the practice, asserting that allowing jurors to decide the law undermined the fundamental principle of legal precedent.[3] And in the decades before the turn of the century, supreme courts in several states ruled against the practice, some quite forcefully. In 1870 the Georgia Supreme Court declared that while the state recognized that jurors in criminal cases were judges of the law and the facts, they had to apply the law they were given by the court.[4] Four years later, that court ruled in one case that it was not a reversible error for a trial judge to refuse to instruct the jurors that they were the judges of the law

[2] *Kane v. Pennsylvania*, 89 Pa. 522, 527 (1879); Francis Wharton, "Disputed Questions of Criminal Law," *Southern Law Review* (new series), 5 (1879): 352, 363–364.
[3] Decius S. Wade, "Jurors as Judges in Criminal Law," *Criminal Law Magazine* 3 (1882): 484, 492–493.
[4] *Brown v. Georgia*, 40 Ga. 689, 697 (1870).

and, in a second case, that it was reasonable for a judge to instruct the jurors that "it is presumed that the court is familiar with the law and you ought to pay deference to those opinions and not contemptuously disregard them."[5] In 1885 the Georgia Supreme Court rejected the line of cases that recognized jurors could judge the facts and the law in criminal trials.[6] Other state courts took a similar stance: in the 1870s, Alabama declared that jurors could judge only the facts, not the law; the Louisiana Supreme Court did the same thing in the 1880s; the supreme courts in Connecticut and Vermont did the same in the 1890s.[7] But states still held out; Illinois continued to recognize that jurors were the judges of the law until 1931.[8]

A more effective means of checking the power of juries and reducing the uncertainty that their haphazard verdicts created was the plea bargain. At the start of the nineteenth century, judges in criminal trials discouraged defendants from pleading guilty, and guilty pleas, when they were allowed, did not result in a negotiated reduction of the sentence. In one famous case in 1804, a Massachusetts court refused to accept a defendant's attempt to plead guilty to a murder charge when he first made the request. The court reminded him that pleading guilty would subject him to the mandatory punishment for his crime – death – and ordered him to take time to reconsider. When he persisted in the request after a period of reflection, the court again reminded him that the consequence of his plea was execution and then allowed the plea; he was hanged

---

[5] *Edwards v. Georgia*, 53 Ga. 428, 432–433 (1874); *Hooper v. Georgia*, 52 Ga. 607, 612–613 (1874).

[6] *Ridenhour v. Georgia*, 75 Ga. 382 (1885).

[7] *Washington v. Alabama*, 63 Ala. 135 (1879); *Louisiana v. Vinson*, 37 La. Ann. 792 (1885); *Vermont v. Burpee*, 65 Vt. 1 (1892); *Connecticut v. Main*, 69 Conn. 123 (1897).

[8] *Illinois v. Butler*, 343 Ill. 146 (1931).

not long after.[9] In that case, the court's repeated warnings to the defendant made it clear that his plea of guilty could not be offered in exchange for a reduced sentence. A few years later, Massachusetts courts did begin to allow defendants to plead guilty in exchange for lighter sentences in cases involving regulatory crimes like liquor violations. The practice began around 1808; by 1845 it had become so widespread that a committee was appointed by the Massachusetts House of Representatives to review the process. That committee endorsed the practice as a reasonable exercise of prosecutorial discretion, and not long after, plea agreements were adopted in the Massachusetts felony courts. The first plea bargain involving murder in Massachusetts took place in 1848; in the 1850s, only 17 percent of all murder cases in Massachusetts were pleaded out. But by the end of the 1890s, 61 percent of all murder cases in Massachusetts were resolved with pleas. Courts in other states also adopted the practice. In Philadelphia between 1895 and 1901, 58 percent of the ninety-two people convicted of murder ended their cases with a plea. A variety of factors made plea agreements attractive and popular. In states like Massachusetts, where judges were appointed, the judiciary resisted the turn to plea bargaining until pressure from caseloads forced their hand. In contrast, in states like Georgia, where judges were elected, the plea bargain was embraced more quickly, as judges used the device to control their caseload and demonstrate their competence to the electorate. Plea agreements were also a means by which all parties to a criminal trial could control the uncertainty of a trial and avoid the possibility of a runaway jury. They offered prosecutors a conviction; they gave criminal defendants, especially defendants whose offense or nationality raised the possibility of juror

[9] *Commonwealth v. Battis*, 1 Mass. 95 (1804).

prejudice, a degree of certainty that a trial could not provide. At the same time, the plea agreements made a mockery of the careful statutory schemes and criminal laws passed by legislatures, since they gave the parties to a suit a way to negotiate an individual punishment that avoided the statutory sanctions for a crime.

RULE OF LAW AND THE COURTS

By the end of the nineteenth century, there were issues of fairness at all layers of the criminal justice system. A murder trial in California suggests that in the felony courts many of those challenges arose as the criminal justice system grappled with incorporating and controlling newly freed people, immigrants, and, to some extent, women. In 1875 Chin Mook Sow, an émigré from China, went on trial in San Francisco, charged with murdering another Chinese immigrant.[10] There were problems from the start; San Francisco, and California, were in the midst of a significant anti-immigration campaign that targeted the Chinese. In 1877 the U.S. Senate held a special investigation into Chinese immigration in China that helped lead to the passage of the Chinese Exclusion Act of 1882.[11] Two years later, California, which already had a number of anti-Chinese laws, adopted a new constitution that contained several anti-Chinese provisions.[12] More immediately, in Chin's case the anti-Chinese sentiments made it hard to find unbiased jurors, a problem that the prosecution exacerbated when it challenged even white jurors who lived near Chinese or had Chinese servants. Matters

[10] *California vs. Chin Mook Sow*, No. 10, 232, Appellate Court File, California State Archives.
[11] *Report of the Joint Special Committee to Investigate Chinese Immigration* (1877); 22 Stat. 58 (1882).
[12] California Constitution of 1879, Art. XIX.

did not improve when the testimony began. Lawyers questioned whether the Chinese witnesses could be trusted to take their oath seriously or testify truthfully. The main witness for the state, a white police interpreter who testified about the dying declaration of the victim, did not speak or understand the Chinese dialect of the defendant or his alleged victim. Several of the prosecution's witnesses admitted they found it hard to tell Chinese men apart.

None of this was unusual; in the nation's increasingly polyglot communities, problems of prejudice were often exacerbated by failures of communication. Those problems of communication posed a particular challenge to the criminal justice system at the end of the nineteenth century. Police could not understand statements made by non-English speaking victims, witnesses, or suspects. Defense attorneys had a hard time communicating with, or advising, their clients. At trial, jurors struggled to make sense of translations offered by court interpreters, who were often asked to try to translate languages or dialects they did not know. And these failures of communication were easily compounded by judicial intransigence. In Chicago, in 1885, three immigrant defendants were convicted of murder on the basis of questionable translations by interpreters who admitted that their Italian was rusty and they were unfamiliar with the Sicilian dialect the defendants spoke. But when attorneys for the defendants tried to present expert testimony to show the jurors that there were significant differences between the Italian the interpreters claimed to understand and the Sicilian dialect the defendants spoke, the trial judge refused to let the attorneys present the evidence.

The right to counsel was still not universal in the late nineteenth century, and concerted efforts to provide attorneys for poor defendants were not made until around World War I. Even then the process took time. In 1914 Los Angeles was the first city to create an office of public defender; three years later, New York created a voluntary organization to represent criminal defendants. Many other jurisdictions waited until the late 1920s and early 1930s to provide counsel for attorneys who could not afford it; other states, like Florida, waited even longer. But judges in several states ordered lawyers to work for free to represent defendants who faced serious charges, and in 1883 the Illinois Supreme Court ruled that an immigrant defendant who was unfamiliar with the American legal system and the English language had a right to have a lawyer appointed.[13] Chin Mook Sow had legal assistance at his trial; weeks before the case went to trial, the judge appointed two attorneys, both leaders in the San Francisco bar, to represent him. They mounted a vigorous defense at his trial; when the jury returned a verdict finding Chin guilty, they filed a lengthy appeal on his behalf.

In their appeal they made two constitutional arguments. Neither was successful, but they are noteworthy as early instances of a rights-based approach that became increasingly popular among some defense attorneys in the last decades of the nineteenth century. In Chin's case the first rights-based argument rested on the Sixth Amendment; his attorneys claimed that by admitting the victim's dying declaration into evidence, the trial judge denied Chin's constitutionally protected right to confront witnesses. That argument was clearly barred by the Supreme Court's decision in *Barron v. Baltimore* (1833) and was summarily dismissed by the trial judge. Their second argument, which challenged the composition of the jury that tried the case, was a more complicated claim that fit an older legal principle into a newer, constitutional framework. At the start

---

[13] *Gardner v. Illinois*, 106 Ill. 76 (1883) (non-English-speaking defendant should have been given a lawyer and a translator before being allowed to plead guilty).

of the trial, Chin's lawyers demanded that he be given a mixed jury, with half its members Chinese. The mixed jury, more formally known as a jury *de mediatate linguae*, was an English institution that had been created by statute during the reign of Edward III. In its earliest guise, the mixed jury was designed to protect foreign merchants by guaranteeing them a jury that was half Englishmen and half people of their own background. Originally, the practice was intended to create a jury with some knowledge of foreign practices and customs. Over time the mixed jury also helped to guarantee that defendants would be tried by a jury that contained some people who understood their native language. English settlers brought the practice to the American colonies, where mixed juries were used when Native Americans and non-English defendants were brought to trial in colonial courts. The use of mixed juries continued after ratification of the Constitution; in 1823 Chief Justice John Marshall, sitting as a trial judge on a federal court, granted a defense request for a mixed jury in a trial for piracy.[14] But the practice fell into disuse; in 1867 the U.S. attorney general issued an opinion declaring that there was no right to a jury *de mediatate linguae* in the United States.[15]

After the Civil War, attorneys for blacks, Native Americans, and immigrants led efforts to revive the practice and tie it to the constitution.[16] In its new manifestation, the argument for a mixed jury rested on the equal protection clause of the recently ratified Fourteenth Amendment. Because that amendment explicitly governed

---

[14] *United States v. Cartacho*, Case No. 14,738 (1823), discussed in *United States v. Carnot*, 25 Fed. Case 297, 297–298 (D.C.C., 1824).

[15] Henry Stanberry, "Opinion in Warren's Case," *Official Opinions of the Attorneys General of the United States* (1867), 12: 319.

[16] See, e.g., *Missouri v. Brown*, 119 Mo. 527 (1894) (African American defendant); *Nevada v. Ah Chew*, 16 Nev. 50 (1881) (Chinese immigrant).

the conduct of state governments, the limitations of *Barron v. Baltimore* did not apply. But while the Supreme Court of the United States recognized, in the abstract, that jurors could not be excluded because of their race (a category that in the late nineteenth century included what we would now consider ethnicity), it refused to hold that courts had an affirmative duty to make sure that juries were racially mixed. And so those claims were usually denied.[17]

PUNISHMENTS

Chin Mook Sow's case ended after his appeal and request for a pardon were denied.[18] In earlier years, public officials had used pardons to mitigate the severity of punishments and display the power of their office. But by the end of the nineteenth century, the pardoning power was on the wane. Sometimes requests for pardons were supplanted by criminal appeals, but governors also were more inclined to defer to the decisions of jurors rather than use the pardon power. So Chin Mook Sow was hanged, just as Joshua Nettles had been more than seventy years before, but there was a difference. California, like several other states, outlawed public hangings in the middle of the century, and in 1866 San Francisco moved all executions into the courthouse of the local jail. After that, people in San Francisco had to get special invitations from the county sheriff to see an execution. Fortunately for those who wished to make sure justice was done, invitations to a hanging were relatively easy to come by and several hundred people were able to watch Chin die in 1879.

---

[17] *Strauder v. West Virginia*, 100 U.S. 303 (1880); *In re Woods*, 140 U.S. 278 (1891) (African American).

[18] *California v. Chin Mook Sow*, 51 Cal. 597 (1877).

The second half of the nineteenth century saw two other changes in executions. In 1879 the Supreme Court of the United States approved the Utah Territory's decision to use a firing squad to execute those convicted of capital crimes.[19] The Court declared that the practice did not amount to cruel and unusual punishment. In 1890 the mechanics of death took on yet another form when William Kemmler was put to death on the electric chair by the state of New York. Nine years after Kemmler was the first person to be electrocuted, Martha Place became the first woman to die in the electric chair. Other states followed New York's lead. Ohio adopted the electric chair in 1897; three other states (Massachusetts, New Jersey, and Virginia) did so in the first decade of the twentieth century.

Executions were not, of course, the only sort of punishment available. The success of the penitentiary model was firmly established after the Civil War when South Carolina and Florida finally built penitentiaries in 1866. And most states continued to seek profits from their prisoners in the second half of the nineteenth century. Illinois maintained its modified convict leasing system until organized labor forced through a law barring prison work in 1903. Other states, located mostly in the South, began to lease prisoners out to private enterprises, much as Missouri had done in the antebellum period. Florida, which had tried and failed to make a profit on the penitentiary that it finally built, began to lease out its prisoners to turpentine farmers, phosphate mine owners, and railroad companies in 1877 and continued that practice through World War 1. Tennessee and Alabama leased their prisoners to coal mining concerns, and initially both states found the process quite lucrative. By 1866 each state was bringing in $100,000 a year from prisoner leases, a sum that represented one-third of their

---

[19]   99 U.S. 130 (1879).

respective budgets. But as time went on, problems arose. Tennessee in particular had difficulties when nonconvict miners rioted and forced coal mining companies to release their prisoners and close down their mines. Alabama's experiment with convict miners was slightly more successful, and the state used convicts, particularly African Americans, in its mines for several years. But Alabama's system was subject to free-labor protests as well and worked only so long as the mining companies were willing to give the convict miners pay and privileges. When that arrangement broke down, the convict miners refused to produce and the enterprise became less profitable.

Other southern states, beginning with Georgia in 1866, shifted away from leasing out their inmates and instead put them on chain gangs to do public work. The chain gang was not a southern invention; from 1786 to the opening of Walnut Street Jail in 1790, convicts in Philadelphia were assigned to gangs that did public labor on the streets of the city, wearing a ball and chain to mark their status. In the 1840s, San Francisco housed prisoners on a prison ship, the *Euphemia*, at night and assigned them to do public works in chain gangs during the day. Nor did the chain gang spring fully formed from Georgia soil at the end of the Civil War. Initially, the state assigned misdemeanor arrestees to the chain gang and leased its felony convicts out to private enterprise. The passage of time and problems with the private sector convinced the government of the benefits of having all its convicts work the chain gang to build public roadways, and in 1908 Georgia passed a law that prohibited convict leasing and put all its prisoners (including women, who served as cooks) on gangs. Other states, among them North and South Carolina, followed Georgia's lead, assigning some inmates to a variety of public works projects. That practice continued well into the twentieth century.

The years after the Civil War saw another development in imprisonment, as specialized prisons were built to deal with specific populations. Once again, this was not an entirely new idea. The first house of refuge, a special institution for juvenile offenders, opened in New York in 1825. Twenty years later, Boston offered a refinement of this principle when it opened the first reform school for boys. The first reform school for girls, the Massachusetts State Industrial School for Girls, did not open until 1856, and it was not until after the Civil War that other states, among them Wisconsin, Iowa, Michigan, and Kentucky, created similar institutions. They did not, however, all follow the same model. When the Louisville, Kentucky, House of Refuge opened in 1864 its inmates were boys and girls. In contrast, when the Girls Reform School of Iowa opened in 1866 it was, as its name implied, a single-sex institution. Not only did the Michigan Reform School for Girls, which opened in 1884, have an inmate population that was limited to young women, but its entire staff was female as well.

While these institutions physically separated some young inmates from adult convicts, far more young offenders were housed with older criminals. Even after the Civil War, offenders younger than twenty-one made up a portion, sometimes a significant one, of the populations of penitentiaries and county jails. In 1870 California state courts assigned boys as young as twelve to fifteen to San Quentin and Folsom prisons. Of the 7,566 people assigned to Cook County Jail (in Chicago) in 1882, 508 were younger than sixteen (one was no older than eight); 1,413 were under twenty-one. In the 1890s, a Savannah, Georgia, newspaper reported that one-third of the people assigned to the local penitentiary were younger than twenty, and eighty of them were less than fifteen years old. Nor were juvenile offenders exempt from the profit motive that drove corrections. In Tennessee, juveniles, who were not segregated from adult inmates, were expected to earn their keep by their labor, just as adults were. The same was true for juvenile offenders in jurisdictions that did separate them from the general prison population. Inmates in the New York House of Refuge were contracted out to private businesses or expected to do contract labor within the House itself. Inmates at the Michigan Reform School were also contracted out to private business. Similar things happened at the reformatories opened for women offenders. The Detroit House of Refuge, a reformatory for women, ran a successful chair manufacturing business in the early 1870s.

Reformers, particularly women, had lobbied states to create all-women cell blocks and to hire women as matrons for women prisons as early as the 1820s. Some states built special reformatories for women prisoners in the middle of the nineteenth century, but for much of the century women were assigned to the same penitentiaries as men. The Old Louisiana State Penitentiary, which functioned from the 1830s to 1918, held male and female prisoners (and a number of the prisoners' children) throughout most of its history. Illinois housed female inmates (less than 3 percent of its prison population) in the penitentiary at Joliet until it finally opened a women's prison in 1896. Few states took the situation of women inmates seriously in the late nineteenth century; Missouri appropriated money for a women's prison in 1876 but neglected to build one until 1926. Idaho did not even create a women's ward in its penitentiary until 1905 and did not build a women's prison until 1974. In contrast to those states that assigned women to penitentiaries along with men, Massachusetts housed its female prisoners in the county jails until it created the Reformatory Prison for Women in 1875. One reason for the delays in creating separate women's prisons was economic: prisons and prison industries relied on female inmates to do their housekeeping.

The first completely separate prison for women (actually a reformatory, not a penitentiary) opened in Indiana in 1873. A few years later, in 1877, the first reformatory for men aged thirty years or younger opened in Elmira, New York. In theory, reformatories were intended to rehabilitate inmates by educating them and training them for useful work. To that end, inmates at Elmira were graded on their conduct and placed in different classes based on their behavior, with the idea of gradually preparing them to return to the outside world. In practice, however, things were much as they were in penitentiaries. Elmira's first director, Zebulon Brockway, had previously been the director at the Detroit House of Corrections, where he had been noted for turning a profit with the prison's chair manufacturing business. He brought the profit motive with him to Elmira, where inmates soon found that they spent an entire workday in the reformatory's several factories and spent only an hour and a half in the evening at the specially designed classrooms.

Although reformatories boasted a range of services for their inmates, the greatest differences between the penitentiary and the reformatory were more basic. One had to do with what brought the inmates to the reformatories in the first place. While some were imprisoned for committing crimes, many, especially women and children, were imprisoned on more amorphous grounds – appearing immoral, having drunken parents, or being incorrigible. The other had to do with sentences. Inmates at reformatories typically had indeterminate sentences so that they could work their way out of incarceration. In practice, however, as Samuel Walker has demonstrated, sentences given to inmates at reformatories typically lasted longer than those given to people sentenced to penitentiaries. That was because of two other reforms of law. In the first part of the nineteenth century, those sentenced to a penitentiary might see their sentence reduced by a governor's pardon. After 1850, a number of states passed good-time laws that allowed prison officials to reduce inmates' sentences for good behavior. The practice of parole, by which inmates whose behavior had been good were released so long as they remained subject to the oversight of a parole board or some other institution that monitored their behavior and could restore them to prison if they violated parole, provided another way for inmates to get out of penitentiaries before their sentence was completed.

CENTRALIZING POWER

During the Civil War, the federal government began to take a more serious interest in criminal justice. In the first years of the war, Congress created military tribunals, which tried civilians for a number of offenses. In their initial manifestation, those courts heard charges of treason and sabotage, but as time passed their jurisdiction expanded and by war's end those courts were hearing cases that covered everything from morals offenses to fraud. The Civil War increased federal law enforcement power in other ways as well. In 1861 Allen Pinkerton's detective agency, which had previously conducted investigations for businesses, was hired to serve as the secret service for the Union Army. Over time, the agency's role expanded as Pinkerton's investigated businesses accused of defrauding the government, hunted down Confederate spies, and monitored enemy troop strength. Pinkerton's was not the only agency doing law enforcement work during the Civil War. In 1862 Congress established the Bureau of Internal Revenue and gave it the power to investigate and enforce tax laws.[20] At roughly the same time, Congress authorized funds to pay

[20] 12 Stat. 432 (1862).

for a private police force under the control of the secretary of the interior. That became the Secret Service, and was made a permanent agency and transferred to the control of the secretary of the treasury in 1865. The federal government had another, super police force at its disposal, as the army fulfilled a policing function in the states of the former Confederacy in the period between 1865 and 1870. The army served as police above the Mason Dixon Line as well, especially during the nationwide strike in 1877. In 1878, in the Posse Comitatus Act, Congress formally declared that the armed forces should not be involved in enforcing criminal laws.[21] But that did not completely end the military's policing role, since the army could still be called in to serve as a police force during national emergencies. In the last years of the nineteenth century, that meant the army was activated during labor struggles.

Congress also signaled a greater willingness to intervene in state criminal procedures in 1867, with passage of the Habeas Corpus Act.[22] That law provided that the writ could be used for review of state or federal court convictions, a provision that, at least in theory, gave the judges in federal courts the power to sit in review of some state court criminal trials. Congress also expanded the federal reach into criminal law by increasing the number of federal crimes. Initially, as it had in the past, it limited those laws to areas under federal jurisdiction. In 1860 Congress passed a law that was intended to protect immigrating women from seduction on board ship.[23] Two years later it passed the Morrill Anti-Bigamy Act, another piece of morals legislation that declared polygamy a crime in federal territories.[24] In 1885, in response to the Supreme Court's

---

[21] 20 Stat. 152 (1876).
[22] 14 Stat. 385 (1867).
[23] 12 Stat. 3 (1860).
[24] 12 Stat. 501 (1862).

opinion in *Ex parte Crow Dog* (1883), which held that in the absence of a federal law, the federal courts lacked jurisdiction to hear trials of crimes committed in Indian Territory, Congress passed the Major Crimes Act.[25] That Act gave the federal courts the power to hear cases involving major crimes (such as murder, rape, or theft) committed on Indian reservations.

In the last decades of the nineteenth century, Congress also moved aggressively to federalize some aspects of substantive criminal law using a number of constitutional provisions to do so. It relied on its powers under the Thirteenth and Fourteenth Amendments to pass the Civil Rights Act of 1866.[26] It relied on those amendments again in the 1870s when it passed the so-called Force Acts. The first of those laws, the Force Act of 1870, made it a crime to use threats or force to prevent people from voting.[27] The next year, Congress passed the Force Act of 1871, sometimes known as the Ku Klux Klan Act, which created criminal penalties for those, like members of the Klan, who attacked blacks and their white allies.[28] Another force act, also known as the Civil Rights Act of 1875, made it a crime to deprive citizens of the "full and equal enjoyment of the accommodations, advantages, facilities, and privileges of inns, public conveyances on land and water, theaters, and other places of public amusement" based on their race.[29] Freed from the sectional pressures that had checked its efforts to pass morals legislation before the Civil War, Congress also passed a variety of laws of that sort. In 1873 it relied on its constitutional authority to regulate the mail to pass the Comstock Act, which made it a crime to send obscene

[25] 109 U.S. 556 (1883); 23 Stat. 385 (1885).
[26] 14 Stat. 27 (1866).
[27] 16 Stat. 140 (1870).
[28] 17 Stat. 13 (1871).
[29] 18 Stat. 335 (1875).

materials, including information related to contraception, through the mail.[30] In 1895 it passed the Lottery Act, which was based on Congress's power to regulate commerce.[31] Congress relied on the commerce clause to justify other laws with criminal elements, including the Sherman Antitrust Act of 1890 and the Erdman Act of 1898, which made it a federal offense for an employer engaged in interstate commerce to blacklist or fire employees who joined a union.[32]

While Congress was more than eager to act in the area of criminal law in the late nineteenth century, the Supreme Court was not often willing to endorse the practice. In *United States v. Kajama* (1886), the Court upheld the Major Crimes Act of 1885, declaring that it was a legitimate exercise of Congress's plenary powers to legislate over territorial lands and regulate the Indian nations.[33] But while it was willing to endorse congressional action over the territories, the Court was not so eager to embrace restrictions on state power. Often, its rulings turned on the impact of the law on state police powers, and its decisions there were as confusing as they had been in the antebellum era. In the *Civil Rights Cases* (1882), for example, the Court struck down part of the Civil Rights Act of 1875, on the ground that it infringed on the police powers of the states.[34] Then in *United States v. Harris* (1883), a case arising out of a brutal lynching in Tennessee, the Court struck down part of the Force Act of 1871 on the ground that its restrictions on private conduct made it a criminal law and neither the Thirteenth nor the Fourteenth Amendments gave Congress the power to enact criminal

[30] 17 Stat. 598 (1873).
[31] 28 Stat. 963 (1895).
[32] 26 Stat. 209 (1890); 30 Stat. 424 (1898).
[33] 118 U.S. 375 (1886).
[34] 109 U.S. 3 (1882).

laws.[35] A decade after it decided the *Civil Rights Cases* and *Harris*, the Court seemed to confirm their logic when it struck down parts of the Sherman Antitrust Act in *United States v. E. C. Knight* (1895).[36] In *E. C. Knight* the Court declared that the state's police powers were "essentially exclusive," which suggested the possibility that the federal government had, at best, a very limited role in the area of criminal law. But that same year, in *In re Debs* (1895) the Court upheld a federal contempt proceeding arising out of a federal injunction against the railroad boycott and justified the result with reference to the congressional authority to regulate mail and interstate commerce.[37] The Court added that while the government of the United States was a government of limited power, it had full sovereignty within the powers it had been granted, which certainly seemed to indicate that the federal government could play a significant role in criminal justice, so long as it grounded its efforts in specific constitutional provisions. And that is more or less what happened. As William Forbath has noted, after *Debs* the federal courts claimed the power to overrule decisions by state authorities, even in the area of criminal justice.[38]

The Supreme Court's decisions regarding the rights of defendants in federal criminal trials were more consistent, and often revealed more sympathy for arguments that tried to expand protections granted to defendants in federal criminal trials. In *Coffin v. United States* (1895) the Court held that the presumption of innocence was a fundamental element of Western legal traditions and reversed a verdict in a federal bank fraud case on the

[35] 106 U.S. 629 (1883); 16 Stat. 140 (1870).
[36] 156 U.S. 1 (1895).
[37] In re Debs, 158 U.S. 564 (1895).
[38] W. Forbath, *Law and the Shaping of the American Labor Movement* (1991), 101, 106.

ground that the trial judge's instructions failed to properly advise the jurors of the presumption and its implications.[39] The next year, in *United States v. Bell* (1896),
the Court defined the scope of the Fifth Amendment's
double jeopardy protection for federal defendants when
it held that a defendant who had been tried and acquitted
on an indictment that was later discovered to be defec-
tive could not be retried.[40] Although it showed a greater
willingness to recognize that the provisions of the Bill of
Rights gave defendants in federal criminal cases procedural protections, the Court continued to resist attempts
to extend those protections to state court trials. In 1866,
in *Pervear v. Massachusetts*, a defendant convicted in
state court for selling alcohol appealed his conviction to
the Supreme Court of the United States, claiming that
his sentence, a fine of $50 and three months of hard
labor, was cruel and unusual punishment in violation of
the Eighth Amendment.[41] The Supreme Court rejected
his claim, citing its opinion in *Barron v. Baltimore*. It
repeated that point at the very end of the century, in
Brown v. New Jersey (1899), where it held that the "first
ten Amendments to the federal Constitution contain no
restrictions on the powers of the states."[42]

While the attorneys for the defendant in *Pervear*, like
the attorneys for Chin Mook Sow in California, relied
simply on the Bill of Rights to make their claims, counsel
for other defendants offered more complicated versions
of that claim. In *Hurtado v. California* (1884), the defendant was found guilty of murder and sentenced to death.[43]
On appeal to the Supreme Court, his attorneys argued

[39] 156 U.S. 432 (1895).
[40] 163 U.S. 662 (1896).
[41] 72 U. S. 475 (1866).
[42] 175 U.S. 172, 175 (1899).
[43] 110 U.S. 516 (1884).

that the proceedings against him, specifically the decision to charge him on an information as opposed to bringing him before the grand jury, violated the Fifth Amendment, which they claimed applied to states like California through the Fourteenth Amendment's requirement of due process. The Court refused to accept that argument, concluding that "any legal proceedings enforced by public authority, whether sanctioned by age or custom, or newly devised in the discretion of legislative power, in furtherance of the general public good, which regards and preserves [the] principles of liberty and justice, must be held to be due process of law."[44] It reiterated that point in *Spies v. Illinois* (1887).[45] The Court also continued its earlier practice, set out in *Scott v. Sanford*, of using rights to create different categories of citizens. In *Minor v. Happersett* (1874), the Court held that the equal protection clause of the Fourteenth Amendment did not give women the right to vote.[46] The Court explained that citizenship for women entailed different sorts of rights than did citizenship for men.

At the very end of the century, the Supreme Court joined the state courts in the struggle to stop jurors from deciding the law. The author of that attack on jury power is more than a little surprising. In *Hurtado* Justice John Marshall Harlan wrote a stinging dissent, arguing that the jury was a vital bulwark against government overreach and unjust prosecution. *Hurtado*, of course, involved the question of whether there was a right to a grand jury, but Harlan's language was far more sweeping and encompassed petty juries as well. Yet a decade later, writing for the majority of the Supreme Court in *Sparf and Hansen v. United*

[44] 110 U.S. at 537.
[45] 123 U.S. 131 (1887).
[46] 88 U.S. 162 (1874).

States (1895), Justice Harlan declared that jurors in federal criminal trials could not substitute their view of the law for that given them by the judge.[47]

ROUGH JUSTICE

As the state and federal efforts to stop jurors from deciding the law in criminal cases suggest, the decades after the Civil War were a period of significant transformation of popular justice. But while the courts began to make some headway in their attempt to check jurors' power to substitute justice for law, their efforts were not absolutely successful. In unwritten law cases, jurors continued to excuse men and women who claimed they killed seducers and adulterers. Some juries continued to ignore the law, sometimes encouraged by judges who urged them to follow their common sense rather than legal principles. The practice of jury nullification was most obvious in cases where defendants invoked unwritten law to justify their decisions to kill others, but New York City prosecutor Arthur Train complained that juries in criminal trials routinely ignored the law when presented with an insanity defense. The problem was not simply the effect of the practice on individual trials; the legal scholar and reformer Roscoe Pound went further, blaming judges who urged jurors to follow their common sense for creating a general contempt for law.[48] But newspapers, even otherwise conservative papers, applauded jurists who encouraged juries to put their sense of justice above "legalism." Popular forces continued to seek to influence the legal system in other ways. Participants in indignation meetings loudly

---

[47] 156 U.S. 51 (1895).
[48] Roscoe Pound, "Law in Books and Law in Action," *American Law Review* 44 (1910): 12, 16–17, 18.

denounced the course of police investigations or criminal trials, and mobs gathered outside courthouses to express their displeasure over verdicts.

In other respects extralegal forces seemed to be on the ascendant. The last decades of the nineteenth century were marked by a struggle between violent extralegal forces, the lynch mobs that Michael Pfeifer has called enactors of "rough justice," and the advocates of the rule of law.[49] But with the exception of New England, where the most extreme forms of rough justice had been eradicated, popular forces around the country continued their efforts to police their communities and punish those who transgressed. As had been the case before the Civil War, the popular forces of justice sometimes competed with the formal institutions of law, other times claimed to supplement them, and on more than a few occasions acted in concert with government authorities.

Notwithstanding the State's efforts to expand the police and other institutions of formal law in the last decades of the nineteenth century, the roughest forms of popular justice thrived. The years after Reconstruction were marked by the rise of lynching. From the 1880s to the 1930s, lynch mobs killed roughly 2,700 people, male and female, and 80 percent of those people were black. With the exception of New England, no region of the country was free from this form of violence; most lynchings took place in Louisiana, but mobs lynched people in Wisconsin, Pennsylvania, Illinois, and Iowa. And lynch mobs claimed to act for any number of reasons. In December 1874, a mob in Polk County, Iowa, lynched Charles Howard for murder. Four years later, in October 1878, another mob lynched two men, Billy Mansfield and Archie McLaughlin,

[49] Michael Pfeifer, *Rough Justice: Lynching and American Society, 1874–1947* (2006).

for robbery in Wyoming. Then two years after that, a mob in Northampton County, Pennsylvania, lynched Edward Snyder, who was suspected of murdering a local couple, and in June 1882 a mob in California lynched Incanación García for murderous assault. Some mobs in Louisiana, Iowa, and Wyoming lynched men suspected of being horse thieves; other mobs in those same states lynched men for suspected rape and undefined sexual offenses.[50] Many lynchings were justified by the claim that the victims had committed some sort of serious crime, but at least a few mobs offered nothing more than a vaguely racial justification. In 1879 a mob in Louisiana lynched George Williams, a black man, for making "threats against a white"; in 1885 another mob in that state lynched William Pierce Mobry, a white man, for defending a black woman from a beating. In 1891 yet another mob in Louisiana lynched John Coyle, a black, for being a "bad negro."

In 1891, when a mob in New Orleans lynched eleven Sicilian immigrants who had been acquitted after being tried for the murder of the local police chief, elites in that city excused the lynching on the ground that the legal system was "lawless." That argument was not uncommon; lynch mobs often claimed that they had to act because the legal system itself was unjust, even lawless – an argument that echoed the justifications of the mob that burned effigies and stoned the Ward house in Louisville in the 1850s. At the same time, lynch mobs and their advocates particularly stressed the need for prompt and harsh punishment of crimes. When W. C. Clifton was lynched in Wyoming in 1903, the mob attached a note to his body that indicated it had acted because the legal system was "too slow."[51] When another mob lynched Charles Woodward that same year,

---

[50] Pfeifer, *Rough Justice*, 156–183.
[51] Pfeifer, *Rough Justice*, 108.

even after he had been tried and found guilty by a court that sentenced him to death, the trial judge excused the mob's action on the ground that it was important that Woodward be punished by the community in which his crime occurred.[52] In 1891 the *Morning Oregonian* went so far as to blame a lynching on a Washington Supreme Court decision. The Supreme Court had reversed a jury verdict and ordered a new trial in a murder case on the ground that the verdict had depended on uncorroborated accomplice testimony and had been entered by a jury that displayed prejudice against the accused. Notwithstanding that, a headline in the *Morning Oregonian* explained that the lynching demonstrated that "the people act when the law fails." The text of the article emphasized that no one in the community condemned the lynch mob.[53] By grounding the rituals and practices of rough justice so firmly in community, these justifications often helped excuse using lynching against outsiders. There were, to be sure, instances when white mobs lynched whites and a handful of instances when black mobs lynched blacks. But most often the targets of lynch mobs were people at or outside the margins of a community – blacks, Italians, Native Americans, Mexicans, or Jews – and they were killed in the name of community control.

Dramatic and deadly as it was, lynching was not the only form of extralegal justice in the years before 1900. This was also the era of the feud. Between 1873 and 1888, the Hatfields battled the McCoys across the Kentucky–West Virginia border; in the 1880s, the Martins fought the Tollivers in Kentucky. In addition, newspapers in these decades were full of tales of vendettas. Often these stories were centered in the South: Louisiana, Tennessee,

---

[52] Pfeifer, *Rough Justice*, 108.
[53] *Morning Oregonian* (Portland), 12 April 1891, 1.

South Carolina, Virginia, Texas, Florida, Alabama, North Carolina, and Georgia. But there were vendettas in the West, in California, the Arizona Territory, and the Indian country in Wyoming. And there were tales of vendettas and other revenge killings in the North, in New York, Illinois, Indiana, Iowa, New Jersey, Illinois, Wisconsin, and Pennsylvania. Those forms of extralegal justice – lynchings, family feuds, and vendettas – involved several people, but individuals also continued to turn to violence to exact justice in the last decades of the nineteenth century. While duels, by and large, finally stopped with the end of the Civil War, murders were still committed in the name of the unwritten law and young men North and South continued to kill one another in punishment for real and imagined slights, and juries still treated them leniently when they were brought to trial. In 1887 a jury in Chicago acquitted Eugene Doherety, who had been accused of killing Nicholas Jones in a fight outside a bar. In the course of rendering its verdict, the jury apparently decided to ignore the evidence that Doherty had been arrested at the scene minutes after the shooting, a recently fired revolver in hand.

Mobs and community groups also continued to render less deadly judgments. Although churches were less likely to sit in judgment on members of their congregations after the Civil War, some churches, notably in Kentucky, continued the practice of informal censure through the 1880s. In Chicago in the 1870s, a mob in one neighborhood burned down a factory that it felt violated city ordinances and harmed the community. In 1887 women in the town of Ellsworth, Illinois, formed a mob and raided a local saloon to protest intemperance. Other mobs, typically composed of men and boys, executed rough justice from South Carolina and Tennessee in the South to Indiana and Wisconsin in the North. Sometimes these mobs responded to a particular problem: in 1886 a mob in

Irving Park, a Chicago neighborhood, drove out of town a man it suspected of taking indecent liberties with children. Other times, mobs were formed to deal with general problems. In the 1880s, communities in Indiana and South Carolina formed groups of "White Caps," bands of men who beat men suspected of whipping or otherwise abusing their wives.

Those rough and ready groups had polite counterparts in the law-and-order leagues and other citizens groups that were formed in several cities. In Chicago in the 1880s, members of the Citizens Association monitored local theaters for shows they considered improper and also watched saloons for liquor law violations. In theory both groups tried to work through official channels, relying on police officers to make arrests; in practice they were perfectly willing to take the law into their own hands, making citizen's arrests when they felt that law enforcement officers were unable, or unwilling, to do so. From 1870 on, New York's Society for the Suppression of Vice worked to close obscene shows, while the city's Anti-Saloon League members monitored and shut down saloons and bars that they felt violated the law. Once again, the actions of these groups reveal the impact of extralegal justice on those at the margins of society. The Anti-Saloon League often focused its attention on working-class bars, while the Committee of Fourteen, yet another law-and-order organization, concentrated its attention on cabarets and saloons that were noted for racial mixing or having a homosexual clientele. To counter that sort of pressure, some extralegal groups were formed to advocate for the excluded. The Committee of Public Safety, established in 1881 in New Orleans, monitored arrests made by the police department, especially when it targeted blacks. The perceived failures of the law in late-nineteenth-century Chicago led small manufacturing concerns and labor organizations to implement their own informal rules of conduct and set up systems for policing their members. Merchants in San Francisco's Chinatown followed a similar course, creating their own private police when the city police department failed to provide them with services and establishing local societies that judged and punished local Chinese. These efforts, though hardly inconsistent with other examples of extralegal justice, were often cited as evidence that immigrants, particularly immigrants from China and southern Italy, were unable to adapt to the rule of law.

CONCLUSION

In the last decades of the nineteenth century, there were significant changes in the area of criminal justice. The increased role of the federal government was the most obvious change, but shifts in methods of punishment marked another area of considerable reform. Those decades were also a period when the ongoing attempts to limit the role of popular forces, particularly juries, in criminal justice finally took hold, although the major means of achieving that goal – the plea bargain – did little to solidify the authority of the sovereign state. At the same time, popular forces of justice, the violent practices of lynching and the more pacific acts of law-and-order leagues, continued to involve the people in the process of judging and punishing and thwarted efforts to establish the rule of law. In the background was a persistent mutter of support for popular or commonsense justice and an attack on the idea of law or legalism from newspapers, politicians, and sometimes even judges.

5

CRIMINAL JUSTICE, 1900–1936

The Supreme Court had largely ignored the problem of mob violence and popular justice through the end of the nineteenth century, but in the first decades of the twentieth century that became harder and harder to do. Still, the Court resisted; not until 1923 did it finally agree that federal courts could intervene to protect the due process rights of defendants tried in state courts amid threats of lynching. That shift was part of a significant, but somewhat haphazard change in direction on the part of the Court as it began to place greater emphasis on the need to protect due process in criminal cases in the years before 1936. The Court was not alone in its increasing concern with popular justice; state governments and Congress also focused more attention on that problem in the first decades of the twentieth century. Yet a variety of factors undermined many of those efforts.

THE SUPREME COURT AND DUE PROCESS

The Supreme Court's gradual shift in attitude began at the start of the new century. In 1906 a black man named Ed

Johnson was arrested and tried in Tennessee on the charge that he had raped a white woman. After his conviction, his lawyers went to federal court with a petition for a writ of habeas corpus, raising two Fourteenth Amendment claims: that blacks had been excluded from the jury pool in his case in violation of the equal protection clause and that the threat of mob violence had intimidated his attorney, preventing Johnson from receiving the sort of legal assistance that due process required. The lower federal courts denied the petition, but the Supreme Court justices agreed that the petition raised significant issues and ordered a hearing. Less than a day after the Court entered that order, a mob marched to the jail that housed Johnson and, with the compliance of the local sheriff, broke in, seized Johnson, and took him away to be lynched. The Supreme Court responded by ordering a contempt hearing; a deputy sheriff and several members of the lynch mob were found guilty and sentenced to prison.[1]

If that aggressive response suggested that the Supreme Court was disturbed by mob violence and popular efforts to subvert trials, subsequent decisions made it clear that the Court was still unwilling to interfere with state court proceedings. In 1915 the Court was presented with another claim that the threat of mob violence in Marietta, Georgia, deprived a defendant charged with rape and murder of his rights to due process.[2] The Court conceded the possibility that popular outrage and the presence of a mob could deprive a defendant of a fair trial, but it concluded that the state court procedures in that particular instance had adequately protected the defendant and allowed him to receive the trial that due process required. The governor of Georgia disagreed and commuted the sentence from death

---

[1] *United States v. Shipp*, 203 U. S. 563 (1908).
[2] *Frank v. Mangum*, 237 U.S. 309 (1915).

to life in prison. Shortly thereafter, a mob organized by political and business leaders in Marietta drove to the state capital, where the defendant was in custody, broke into the jail, seized the defendant, and took him back to Marietta, where they hanged him. Subsequent investigations established conclusively that the victim of that lynching, a local Jewish manufacturer named Leo Frank, was innocent of both the rape and the murder for which he was killed.

The horrific results in the Frank case raised serious questions about the Supreme Court's deference to state court processes, questions the Court did not address until *Moore v. Dempsey* (1923).[3] In that case, which arose out of a murder trial in Arkansas that had been marked by race riots, as well as extended police harassment and abuse of local African Americans, the Court refused to overturn its earlier decision in *Frank*. But the Court did create an exception to *Frank*, declaring that "if the case is that the whole proceeding is a mask – that counsel, jury and judge were swept to a fated end by an irresistible wave of public passion, and that the State Courts failed to prevent the wrong, neither perfection in the machinery for correction nor the possibility that the trial court and counsel saw no other way of avoiding an immediate outbreak of the mob can prevent this court from securing petitioners their constitutional rights."

Moore, where the Court relied on the due process clause to justify its review of the proceedings, was consistent with previous cases from the turn of the twentieth century that demonstrated that the Court considered due process a flexible tool. In *Moyer v. Peabody* (1909), the Court explained that "what is due process of law depends on the circumstances. It varies with the subject-matter and

[3] 261 U.S. 86 (1923).

the necessities of the situation."[4] A decade after it decided *Moore*, the Court again used the due process clause to intervene to protect defendants in a state court criminal trial in *Powell v. Alabama* (1932).[5] *Powell* was an appeal from the Scottsboro trial, where the immediate problem was not the threat of lynching, but the adequacy of the legal representation given to the nine young black men charged with raping two white women. In *Powell*, the Court determined that the due process clause of the Fourteenth Amendment did sometimes include the right to have adequate counsel in capital cases. The Court turned to the due process clause again in *Brown v. Mississippi* (1936), when it held that confessions induced by a beating by police officers could not be admitted at trial.[6] By the 1930s, the Court had become increasingly willing to look more closely at other decisions of state court officers. In 1909, in *Moyer v. Peabody*, the Court upheld the warrantless arrests and detention of individuals during a labor strike on the ground that the governor of the state had declared a state of emergency.[7] The Court suggested that the defendant could have tried to challenge the governor's declaration during a trial, but the Court refused to address the issue where the defendant had not raised it first. Two decades later, in *Sterling v. Constantin* (1932), the Court undertook the inquiry that it avoided in *Moyer v. Peabody*, concluding that the Texas governor's declaration of martial law during a strike was not supported by the evidence.[8]

The Court's flexible understanding of due process meant that it was willing to use the Fourteenth Amendment in other ways as well. In a handful of cases, the Court incorporated

---

[4] 212 U.S. at 84.
[5] 287 U. S. 45 (1932).
[6] 297 U. S. 278 (1936).
[7] 212 U.S. 78 (1909).
[8] 287 U.S. 378 (1932).

rights protected in the Bill of Rights into the due process clause, in order to declare state criminal laws unconstitutional. In a series of cases decided in the early 1930s, the Court incorporated the First Amendment into the Fourteenth Amendment due process clause and struck down laws declaring it a criminal offense to air seditious views, publish malicious libel, and gather.[9] In another line of cases that stretched from *Lochner v. New York* (1905) to *Adkins v. Children's Hospital* (1923), the Court found a right to liberty of contract in the due process clauses of the Fifth and Fourteenth Amendments, and used it to strike down laws that regulated employment relations and imposed punishments for those who failed to comply with those regulations.[10]

At the same time, the Supreme Court continued to expand the rights given to defendants in federal criminal trials. At the very end of the 1930s, in *Johnson v. Zerbst*, the Court held that the Sixth Amendment's right to counsel meant that attorneys should be appointed to represent defendants in federal criminal trials.[11] The Court also began to recognize there were constitutional limits on the punishments that could be meted out to those convicted in the federal courts. In *Weems v. United States* (1910), the Court held that it was cruel and unusual punishment

---

[9] *Stromberg v. California*, 283 U.S 359 (1931) (striking down a law making it a crime to fly the flag of the Communist Party); *Near v. Minnesota*, 283 U.S. 697 (1931) (striking down a law that allowed state courts to enjoin publication of "malicious, scandalous, and defamatory" material); *DeJong v. Oregon*, 299 US. 353 (1937) (striking down a state criminal syndicalism law on the ground it interfered with the right to freedom of assembly); *Lovell v. Griffith*, 303 U.S. 444 (1938); *Hague v. CIO*, 307 U.S. 496 (1939) (striking down a city ordinance that was used to prohibit meetings of labor organizations); *Schneider v. New Jersey*, 308 U.S. 147 (1939) (striking down an anti-littering ordinance that was used to justify arrests of people handing out pamphlets).

[10] *Lochner v. New York*, 198 U.S. 45 (1905); *Adkins v. Children's Hospital*, 261 U.S. 525 (1823).

[11] 394 U.S. 458 (1938).

that violated the Eighth Amendment to sentence a defendant to fifteen years of "hard and painful labor" while being chained at the wrist and ankle.[12] The Court found that the punishment was too extreme for the defendant's crime, falsifying a government document with the intent to defraud. The Court was not so willing to extend the protections of the Constitution to investigation and arrest. One of the Court's most famous cases, *Weeks v. United States* (1914), established the so-called exclusionary rule in federal cases.[13] There, the Court held that a warrantless seizure of papers from a private house violated the Fourth Amendment and declared that the proper remedy for the violation was to exclude those papers from the trial. But in another Fourth Amendment case, *Carroll v. United States* (1925), the Court held that the requirement of a search warrant did not extend to cars, because their mobility made getting a warrant impracticable.[14] Three years later, in *Olmstead v. United States* (1928), the Court held that the Fourth Amendment's requirement of a search warrant did not extend to wiretaps. The Court added that the use of wiretap evidence at a criminal trial did not violate the Fifth Amendment's due process clause. The Court expanded the protections given to criminal defendants in federal courts in nonconstitutional ways as well. In *Sorrels v. United States* (1932), the Court held that defendants were entitled to claim that they had been entrapped into committing a crime by a law enforcement officer.[15] Then in *Valentine v. United States* (1936), the Court held that the president could not extradite U.S. citizens to another country to stand trial in the absence of an act of Congress or a treaty.[16]

[12] 217 U.S. 349 (1910).
[13] 232 U.S. 383 (1914).
[14] 267 U.S. 132 (1925).
[15] 287 U.S. 435 (1932).
[16] 299 U.S. 5 (1936).

While the Court became more willing to conclude that some parts of the Bill of Rights (most notably the provisions of the First Amendment) were incorporated into the due process clause of the Fourteenth Amendment, on the question of whether it would incorporate rights that might protect the claims of criminal defendants in state court proceedings, the Supreme Court held firm. In *Twining v. New Jersey* (1908), the Court reaffirmed its earlier statement that the provisions of the Bill of Rights were not incorporated in the Fourteenth Amendment and that, as a result, criminal defendants on trial in state court could not claim the protections guaranteed in the Bill of Rights at their trial.[17]

CRIMINAL JUSTICE IN THE STATES

Limited as it was, the Supreme Court's newfound concern with criminal procedure and fair trials reflected a larger trend. A number of governments produced studies of the criminal justice system at the turn of the twentieth century. The New York legislature created the Lexan Committee to investigate charges of corruption in the New York City police department in 1894. In 1922 Roscoe Pound and Felix Frankfurter directed the production of a report on criminal justice in the city of Cleveland for the Cleveland Foundation.[18] The Illinois Association for Criminal Justice conducted its own lengthy investigation and published a report in 1929.[19] In the same year President Hoover called for the creation of a federal crime commission to look into criminal justice in the states. The National Commission

[17] 211 U.S. 78 (1908).
[18] *Criminal Justice in Cleveland* (1922).
[19] Illinois Association for Criminal Justice, *The Illinois Crime Survey* (1929).

on Law Observance and Enforcement, better known as the Wickersham Commission, produced a series of investigative reports in 1930 and a final report in 1931. The Wickersham Commission's list of concerns was large, but it focused particularly on problems of policing, including the use of the third degree and other forms of torture and abuse to induce confessions, police misconduct, and police corruption. The Commission claimed that its reports were the first to call attention to the problem of police corruption, but efforts to reform police departments and create police academies, which took off at the turn of the century, were the product of earlier efforts to counter police corruption and misconduct. New York created its training center in 1904, Chicago established one a year later, and the University of California at Berkeley established a training program for the Berkeley Police Department in 1916. Around the same time, reformers in several states pushed for the use of civil service exams in the selection of police officers in order to help prevent corruption.

There were other police reforms in this period. Departments around the country became more sophisticated and extensive in their tracking of data. The Bertillion System of recording descriptions of arrestees had been adopted by a number of police departments in the nineteenth century; in 1904 the St. Louis police department took that practice a step further when it began to take fingerprints of suspects and keep them on file. Over time departments added other kinds of new technology. Cars replaced horse-drawn carriages, while radios and telephones supplanted police call boxes. There was also some effort to change the image and nature of policing, with some departments hiring their first women officers in the years after 1920.

But even with these reforms, police departments came under attack. Police officers were often charged with failing to prevent or properly investigate crimes and were also accused of doing nothing in the face of heightened tension. During the race riots in Chicago in 1919 and Tulsa in 1921, for example, the police were accused of standing by while whites attacked blacks and destroyed their property. During the labor strikes of the era, some charged that the police had carried out gratuitous attacks on striking workers; others accused the police of aiding and abetting the strikers. And to counter those objections, governors often declared a state of emergency and called up national guard units during strikes. That created its own set of problems. During the textile strike of 1933, when workers walked off the job in cotton mills up and down the East Coast, the governor of South Carolina called out the national guard and ordered it to "shoot to kill" any striking worker who tried to enter a cotton mill. During the same strike, the governor of Georgia declared martial law and ordered the national guard to arrest striking workers and hold them for trial in a military tribunal.

For all the talk of reform, the most crucial trend of the late nineteenth century remained unchanged as more and more jurisdictions embraced plea bargains. In 1900 three of four felony convictions in New York county criminal courts resulted from a plea agreement. Within a few years the numbers for other jurisdictions were at least as high. The Illinois Association for Criminal Justice report determined that, in Chicago in the 1920s, 85 percent of all felony convictions resulted from a plea, as did 785 of all felony convictions in Detroit, 76 percent of felony cases in Denver, 90 percent in of felony cases in Minneapolis, 81 percent of felony cases in Los Angeles, 84 percent of felony cases in St. Louis, and 74 percent of felony cases in Pittsburgh.

Plea bargains did not resolve all felony cases, and while those that went to trial resembled the felony trials of the preceding century, they also showed how much trials had changed over the course of a century. In 1901 three men,

Walter McAlister, Andrew Campbell, and William Death, went on trial in New Jersey for the rape and murder of Jennie Bosschieter, a young factory worker (statements at trial described her as either sixteen or seventeen).[20] The men, along with George Kerr, who was tried separately, were accused of drugging Bosschieter with knockout drops in a local saloon and then taking her by cab to a deserted strip of road outside of town, where they raped her. At that point, according to the prosecution, their plan began to unravel. Jennie was unconscious during the rape and did not revive afterward. By the time the panicked men took her back into town and tried to find a doctor to help her, she had died. They took her body back out of town and dumped it near an icehouse, where it was discovered the following day. What happened next demonstrated just how much criminal justice had changed over the course of the nineteenth century. When Elizabeth Cannon awoke with her husband dead beside her, her stepson roused their neighbors; when a worker at the icehouse discovered Bosschieter's body, he phoned the local police. Several officers, including a detective, went to the icehouse, inspected the body and grounds, and then notified the coroner, who summoned a jury to investigate the death. But while that part of the process resembled the investigation into John Cannon's murder, the roles and the actors were quite different. The coroner who was called to the scene was not a local politician or magistrate, but a doctor. The jury he summoned did little more than record the fact that there was a suspicious death, because the real inquiry into Bosschieter's death was undertaken by the coroner and the county medical examiner, who performed the autopsy on her body. And when the autopsy produced no obvious

---

[20] Jonathan Dixon et al., *Trial of Walter C. McAlister, Andrew J. Campbell, and William A. Death for the Murder of Jennie Bosschieter* (1901).

evidence of the causes of her death, the coroner and medical examiner took another step that had no counterpart in the investigation into John Cannon's murder. They carefully removed several organs from Bosschieter's body and sent them to a lab for further tests.

In the meantime, the police officers investigated the crime, aided in this regard by the cab driver, who came forward to implicate some of the men who had been in his cab that night. Policemen went to the houses of those men, arrested them, took them to the stationhouse, and interrogated them. Not long after, several of the men confessed and the defendants were charged on the basis of those confessions. At trial, the confessions were subject to ferocious attack by the defense attorneys, who argued that the police had resorted to a range of behaviors, from promising the suspects leniency if they confessed to physically intimidating the men in order to make them compliant and induce their false confessions. The trial judge ultimately admitted the confessions, which graphically detailed both the rape and the events leading up to Bosschieter's death, but the defense objections probably deserved more attention than they received. The problem of false confessions was not confined to New Jersey; defense counsel and some judges in turn-of-the-century Chicago railed against police efforts to coerce confessions, practices that included holding suspects incommunicado for days in order to induce confessions, as well as using tricks and lies and punishment of the third degree. The Wickersham Commission denounced the police officers' use of the third degree and torture to obtain confessions, and Roscoe Pound argued that the misconduct of the police threatened the entire criminal justice system. The confessions were not the only evidence against the suspects in the McAllister trial, and here again the case demonstrated how much criminal law had changed through the years. In the Nettles and

Cannon trial, the evidence was very local and very personal; it turned on the relationships between the parties and their trustworthiness far more than it explored how the crime might have been committed. The evidence in the McAllister case, in contrast, was focused on proving how the defendants might have killed Jennie Bosschieter. The main expert for the state, a noted chemist, described tests he performed on Bosschieter's stomach, tests that led him to conclude that someone had put chloral hydrate in her drink at the saloon. He concluded that the "Mickey Finn" had killed her. The defense offered the testimony of two other scientific experts. One argued that his tests suggested she had died because she drank too much that night; a second noted that one of the drinks that Bosschieter was supposed to have consumed was absinthe, a notably suspicious drink that could, he asserted, easily kill.

The appearance of expert witnesses was not a new development at trials; English courts had relied on experts before the American Revolution, and throughout the nineteenth century in the United States various sorts of experts had been called to testify about matters that were outside the common knowledge of jurors. Medical and scientific experts had long been part of criminal trials; when Singleton Mercer was tried in New Jersey in 1843 for killing the man who seduced his sister, his lawyers introduced medical and lay witnesses who testified about Singleton's poor health and its effect on his emotions and mental stability. But attitudes toward experts and specialized knowledge had changed between the Mercer and the McAllister trials. In the Mercer case, some of the witnesses who testified about the defendant's mental state were not doctors. The defense argued, and the trial court agreed, that lay witnesses could express an opinion about a person's sanity. At the turn of the twentieth century, lawyers picked experts who had extensive educational attainments and professional experience; during the McAllister trial, all the lawyers made pains to demonstrate just how expert their witnesses were. Yet the twentieth century was also marked by considerable ambivalence about the use of experts at trial. News accounts of trials mocked the hired guns and warring experts who seemed to clutter trials; professional organizations worried about legal attacks on expert witnesses. Experts distrusted jurors, who they felt were not equipped to understand complex testimony; jurors returned the favor and could often be convinced that expert witnesses were trying to obfuscate the facts.

In the McAllister case, the defense attorneys challenged the testimony of the state's experts, hammering away at the uncertainty of their evidence even as they offered their own experts with their own scientific proof and conclusions. But in the end, the deciding factors in the McAllister case were much less complicated. The defense called attention to the fact that Jennie Bosschieter's immigrant parents were used to her staying out late, sometimes even all night, and reminded the jurors that Bosschieter was well known at the saloon where she met the defendants. Having suggested that she was, if not a prostitute, a young woman who was looking for trouble, they cast the defendants as hardworking and responsible white collar workers who had lived blameless lives. And the defense emphasized, over and over again, that none of the medical witnesses who examined Jennie's body had found any evidence that proved she had been raped. The state sought convictions for first degree murder; the defense asked that the defendants be acquitted. Like their counterparts in the Cannon and Nettles case, the jurors at the McAllister trial split the difference. They found the three men on trial guilty of second degree manslaughter; each was sentenced to thirty years in jail. After that, rather than face his own trial, Kerr pleaded guilty to rape and was sentenced to fifteen years.

REFORM OF THE PETTY COURTS

While the trials, North and South, that ended with a lynching raised some doubts about the assertion, cases like the McAllister trial were cited to prove that the felony courts of the turn of the century worked. No one made a similar claim about the petty courts, which handled the bulk of the nation's criminal law cases and notoriously provided little by way of law or justice. By 1910 about 70 percent of all the inmates in the country were serving time for minor offenses like drunkenness, vagrancy, or disorderly conduct, and most of them had been tried and sentenced in a petty court. There was no pretence of due process in these courts. Defendants received a hearing that lasted no more than a minute or two, and while the judges in the petty courts were increasingly likely to have some legal training, there were few lawyers in these courtrooms and less law. The only thing they had in common with the felony courts was indefinite sentencing: many defendants were held overnight following their arrest, then sentenced to time served and ordered to pay a small fine, but since few could afford to pay their fine, they were usually returned to jail after their court appearance and remained there as they worked off their fine. Often these courts were used to target specific types of defendants, who were then charged with particular crimes. In Chicago between 1890 and 1925, vagrancy laws were used against white tramps from out of town. In Pittsburgh in that same period, young African American men from the community were imprisoned under the "tramp law" in numbers far out of proportion to their percentage of the population, while white men were underrepresented. Vagrancy laws were used in Buffalo at the start of the century to break strikes, which meant that most of the men charged and convicted of that offense were local white workers.

Faced with considerable hostility to its disorganized police courts, in 1906 Chicago collapsed them all into a centralized municipal court system. The new court heard petty crimes and handled preliminary hearings, as had the police courts before it. The difference between the old and new systems lay in the way the new courts handled petty cases. Specialized courts were set up to hear particular matters: morals court, for example, heard all the cases involving prostitution and sex crime; gun court heard cases involving weapons. Initially, this specialization reduced the number of cases heard by each judge, which permitted the judges to devote more time and attention to the cases. And for a brief period immediately after the reforms, these courts served as a place where working-class and poor men and women could bring private prosecutions and work to resolve differences. But even in that initial period, the new courts came at a cost to those who appeared before them. The judges in the court had the power to sentence people to indefinite probation and were supported by a phalanx of social workers and social scientists trained in a variety of approaches that included, at least in the period around World War I, eugenics. As a result, the municipal courts quickly became something other than a place where parties aired neighborhood problems and then went home. Women who filed claims against their husbands, parents who used the court to try to control their children, and any defendant brought before the municipal judge in some other way quickly found that the court became a permanent part of their lives. Long after the initial case came to an end, judges, probation officers, and the courts' social science support staff continued to track the parties. Chicago's Juvenile Court was created in 1899. Like the Municipal Court, the new Juvenile Court involved itself in the lives of those who came before it, and its reach was wide. Had Jennie Bosschieter lived in Chicago, she and her parents could easily have come within the purview of the city's new Juvenile Court. Reformers argued that the Juvenile Court's ad hoc judgments, shaped by social science ideals rather than the impersonal rule of law, would protect girls like Jennie. One way the court might have done so was by declaring her a sexual delinquent and sending her to reform school.

Chicago's new courts served as models for reform efforts in other states; by 1920 there were juvenile court systems in most of the states. But although these courts encouraged extended intervention in the lives of the people who appeared before them, the courts were never the perfect creatures of an omnipresent State. In Chicago, government underfunding meant that private individuals and institutions supported (and thus controlled) the Juvenile Court in its first decades. Chicago's Municipal Court was also subject to a variety of competing private influences, as reformers and social scientists played a role in shaping its direction. Because the reformers used the two courts as sites on which to pitch competing ideas, the new courts spoke with several, often inconsistent voices. And just as overburdened dockets had limited the role of earlier police courts as sources of the authority of the State, the competing and conflicting theories drifting out of the Juvenile and Municipal Courts weakened the ability of the state to use either as consistent means of control.

PUNISHMENT IN THE STATES

In many respects, the trends of late-nineteenth-century punishment continued into the twentieth. The defendants in the McAllister case provide an example. Three were sentenced to thirty years in prison, the fourth, who pleaded guilty, to fifteen. Yet because of good-time provisions, none served his full term. There were, however, some efforts at reform. Many states began the new century under pressure from prison reformers like Thomas Mott Osborne and Kate Barnard or muckrakers like Joseph Fishman and Robert Burns.[21] And in some states the reformers' pressure bore fruit. Illinois ended its modified convict leasing system in 1903, when organized labor forced through a law that banned prisoner work, and Kansas stopped trying to make a profit by housing inmates from other states in 1909. But other states resisted the pressure to end the practice of using prisons as a profit center. Missouri continued to do so until 1920, and New Hampshire did not abandon the practice of convict leasing until 1932.

Other reform efforts targeted the death penalty. In 1907 Kansas became the first state to abolish the death penalty since the Civil War. Within the next ten years, six other states followed suit; the last, Missouri, did so in 1917. But several of these reforms were short lived. Two years after it eliminated the death penalty, Missouri reinstated it. By 1920 three of the other states that had abolished the death penalty had reversed themselves. Michael Pfeifer has argued that a commitment to the death penalty was a necessary final step in defeating rough justice, as only the promise that formal processes would replicate the harsh punishment exacted by mobs would persuade communities to give up their extralegal practices.[22] And the backtracking on the death penalty, coupled with the long-term decline of lynching, seems to bear him out. But that does not mean that there were no lynchings in the twentieth century. According to the Tuskegee Institute's records, there were 847 lynchings between 1901 and 1910, 507 between 1911 and 1920, 275

---

[21] Thomas Mott Osborne, *Society and Prisons* (1916); Joseph F. Fishman, *Crucibles of Crime: The Shocking Story of the American Jail* (1923); Thomas E. Burns, *I Am a Fugitive from a Georgia Chain Gang* (1932).

[22] Michael Pfeifer, *Rough Justice: Lynching and American Society, 1874–1947* (2006), 122–123.

between 1921 and 1930, and 112 between 1931 and 1940.
And the practice continued to gain advocates. In the 1890s,
the Georgian populist Tom Watson had urged that lynch
law be made odious so that the practice would end. In 1915
he embraced the practice, explaining that blacks had to be
lynched occasionally to keep them under control. Two years
later Watson added that "lynch law is a good sign: it shows
that a sense of justice yet lives among the people."[23]

ROUGH JUSTICE

While the promise of a stronger, surer death penalty helped
finally defeat the proponents of rough justice, the end of
lynching was also a product of popular forces. African
American newspapers and organizations led anti-lynching
campaigns, using examples like the Leo Frank case to call
attention to the injustice of the practice. At the same time,
local business leaders and elites pushed back against rough
justice, arguing that economic growth and social order
depended on the rule of law and due process.

Other familiar forms of extralegal justice continued in the
twentieth century, though they, too, were increasingly subject to challenge. Labor organizations, from the American
Federation of Labor to the Industrial Workers of the World
(IWW), led boycotts, destroyed property, and struck to press
their claims for economic justice. During World War I, mobs
attacked Germans and pacifists to express their disapproval
and punish them. Race riots, typically justified by vague suspicions of black crime, swept through a number of cities,
North and South, between 1915 and 1921, with white mobs
destroying black-owned property and assaulting blacks. It
never took much to set those incidents off; the Chicago Race
Riot of 1919 began when a gang of white youths attacked

[23] Quoted in C. Vann Woodward, *Tom Watson* (1938), 432–433.

a black who, while swimming, floated into an area of Lake Michigan that had been unofficially declared all white.

Likewise, law-and-order leagues continued to take the law into their own hands. In 1901 Judge William Travers Jerome led members of the New York City Vigilance League on raids of brothels and gambling dens, arguing that citizens had to enforce the laws because the police failed to act. And the Committee of Fourteen, another anti-vice society, targeted cabarets and saloons in New York though the 1920s. As Judge Jerome's participation in the Vigilance League demonstrated, the space between extra-legal justice and popular actions in support of the State sometimes became nearly invisible in the early twentieth century. This was particularly true of labor disputes, where popular forces joined police and government agencies to suppress strikes in a manner that called to mind the old system of community policing and the role of the posse in fugitive slave law cases. When the IWW and Communists organized farm workers in Washington's Yakima Valley in 1933, growers organized vigilante groups that then worked with the national guard to break the strike. During the textile strike that same year, the governor of South Carolina announced he would deputize all citizens of the state to work with law enforcement officers to end the strike. When a strike broke out in a mine in Minnesota in 1934, local businessmen organized as the Committee of Twenty-five called a meeting to create a citizens army to help maintain order; that "army" helped break up the strike.

Although the American Legion denounced all forms of popular justice, Legion locals were often involved in these private and public efforts at social control. During the police strike in Boston in 1919, members of the local American Legion branch joined businessmen and Harvard students in patrols to preserve the peace (and break the strike). Legionnaires in Denver, Colorado, and Youngstown, Ohio,

organized patrols during strikes that same year. Those relatively peaceful activities contrasted with the more violent
anti-labor activities of other Legion posts. In 1929 Legion
members in North Carolina participated in vigilante groups
that led the attack on striking textile workers in Gastonia.
A few years later, members of American Legion posts in
Columbus, Ohio, joined with local law enforcement officers
and, armed with tear gas and machine guns, helped subdue a crowd of striking coal miners intent on freeing some
colleagues who had been arrested. In 1934 some members
of the California American Legion helped disrupt a farm-
workers strike in the Imperial Valley, while others helped
law enforcement officers break up the longshoremen's
strike in San Francisco. That same year, another group of
Legionnaires joined the Aliquippa, Pennsylvania, police
department in an attack on striking steelworkers. While
American Legion posts were particularly active in the area
of labor disputes, local posts engaged in extralegal justice
at other times as well. Many Legion posts were particularly
hostile to radicals or immigrants suspected of having radical views. Some Legion posts convicted radicals at mock
trials and then ran them out of town; other posts tarred
and feathered suspected radicals. But in all these instances
the Legion was quick to claim it was acting to help the government, not to supplant it. Others had a similar take on
the Legion's role, though they took a somewhat dimmer
view of the Legion's activities. Writing about the American
Legion on the eve of its convention in Paris in 1927, an
anonymous correspondent for *L'Humanité* described the
organization as a virtual fourth branch of government.[24]

   The Legion posts and their defenders might not have
appreciated being called the fourth branch of government,
but they did see the Legionnaires who stepped in to help

[24] Brooke L. Blower, *Becoming American in Paris* (2010), 182.

local law enforcement as a semipermanent posse, a modern version of the citizens who organized to help the government keep order and solve crimes. But around the country, from Pennsylvania to California, private companies turned that familiar relationship between public and private actors on its head by creating and controlling company towns. In Aliquippa, Pennsylvania, Jones and Laughlin Steel Company built the schools, owned the waterworks and most of the housing, and controlled the police and local government. The company also employed a private police force to watch for outsiders who might have come into the town to organize workers. Other companies that lacked a town to call their own invested in private police forces; an investigation by the LaFollete Committee found that between January 1934 and June 1936 General Motors spent at least $994,855 on private detectives. None of this was completely new: company towns and private police forces had existed in the nineteenth century. But in the early twentieth century they added to the confusion about where popular justice ended and the State began.

CONGRESS AND CRIMINAL LAW

The horrors of rough justice may have goaded the Supreme Court to act, but they were not enough to influence Congress. Congress first considered an anti-lynching bill in 1909 but was unable to pass it. In 1927 another anti-lynching bill was blocked by senators from southern states. Yet another anti-lynching bill stalled in 1935 when President Roosevelt refused to press for its passage out of fear that doing so would lose him votes in the South in the 1936 election.

In other respects, Congress was active in the field of criminal law between 1900 and 1936. Its work in that area began at the turn of the century. In 1891 Congress authorized the creation of three federal prisons. Over the next fifteen years, those prisons were established at Fort Leavenworth, Kansas (1895), Atlanta (1902), and McNeil Island, Washington (1904). By 1930, when Congress created the Federal Bureau of Prisons, there were five federal prisons, including one that was exclusively for women. Although the federal government had previously managed prisons in federal territories and had established military prisons, these were the first prisons built to deal with those convicted of federal crimes. Before, those convicted in federal courts had been placed in nearby state prisons.

The creation of those prisons heralded an upsurge in federal prisoners. In 1890 the federal government had fewer than 2,000 prisoners; in 1940 there were almost 20,000 federal prisoners. While that number paled in comparison with the number of people in state prisons (145,000 in 1940), the sharp increase in federal prisoners reflected the significant rise in the number of federal crimes. In 1910 Congress passed the Mann Act, which declared it a federal crime to take a woman across state lines for the purpose of prostitution.[25] Not long after, in the midst of anxiety caused by World War I, Congress passed the Espionage Act of 1917 and the Sedition Act of 1918.[26] The former made it a federal crime to disrupt the draft, convey false statements about the military with the intent to disrupt military operations, or try to cause insubordination by those serving in one of the armed forces. The latter made it a felony to disrupt recruiting or enlistment or to publish "disloyal, profane, scurrilous, or abusive language about the form of government." Two years later, Congress passed the Dyer Act, which declared it a federal crime to take a stolen car across state lines.[27] That same year, Congress passed the

[25]   36 Stat. 825 (1910).
[26]   40 Stat. 217 (1917), amended 40 Stat. 533 (1918); 40 Stat. 553 (1918).
[27]   41 Stat. 434 (1919).

Volstead Act, which made it a federal crime to manufacture, transport, or sell alcohol.[28] In 1932 Congress made it a federal crime to cross state lines with a kidnap victim, and in 1934 Congress made kidnapping a capital offense.[29] Another law passed in 1934 regulated the sale of sawed-off shotguns, machine guns, and other "gangster weapons," and made it a felony to fail to comply with regulations.[30] That same year, a third law made it a federal crime to rob a national bank, while a fourth made it a federal crime to flee from one state to another to avoid prosecution for certain felonies.[31] Congress relied on a number of constitutional provisions when it passed those laws. Many, including the Mann Act and Dyer Act, were based on the commerce clause, which established congressional authority to regulate matters in interstate commerce. The Espionage and Sedition Acts were derived from congressional authority over the armed forces, while the Volstead Act was based on the Eighteenth Amendment.

In the twentieth century, the Supreme Court was much more willing to uphold federal criminal laws. It upheld the Lottery Act (1895) in *Champion v. Ames* (1903) and the Mann Act in *Hoke v. United States* (1913), and it affirmed convictions under the Sedition Act in 1919.[32] Considerable confusion underlay the Court's rulings in these opinions. And over the years the Court became more willing to recognize that Congress had police powers. In early cases, like *Adair v. United States* (1908), the Court seemed to echo its decisions from the late nineteenth century, concluding that state police

---

[28] 41 Stat. 305 (1919).
[29] 47 Stat. 781 (1932); 48 Stat. 781 (1934).
[30] 48 Stat. 1236 (1934).
[31] 48 Stat. 782 (1934).
[32] *Champion v. Ames*, 188 U.S. 321 (1903); *Hoke v. United States*, 227 U.S. 308 (1913); *Abrams v. United States*, 250 U.S. 616 (1919); *Schenck v. United States* 249 U.S. 47 (1919).

powers were nearly absolute and could not be supplanted by federal law.[33] But in *Hoke* (1917), the Court explicitly affirmed that Congress had the police power to regulate individual morality under the commerce clause.[34] And in cases like *Coppage v. Kansas* (1915) and *Adkins v. Children's Hospital* (1923), the Court was willing to restrict state police powers when they infringed on private rights protected by the due process clause of the Fourteenth Amendments.[35] By the 1920s, the Court seemed to have rejected the idea that state police powers were absolute and to be well on its way toward recognizing that several different provisions in the Constitution gave Congress police powers.

In the first decades of the twentieth century, Congress also increased the federal government's role in law enforcement. Congress created a Bureau of Investigation in 1908. That bureau was put in the Department of Justice and became the Federal Bureau of Investigation. In 1924 J. Edgar Hoover became the director of the FBI and began his decades-long push to expand the agency's role in criminal justice. Congress gave him a hand, giving the FBI the power to enforce many of the new laws it created in 1934. The FBI also became involved in collecting crime statistics in the 1920s, when it created the Uniform Crime Reporting program. At various times, other federal agencies stepped up their law-enforcing activities as well. During World War I, the postmaster general ordered foreign-language newspapers to submit literal translations of any articles or editorials they published that concerned the U.S. government, the conduct of the war, or the politics of any other nation. During the Red scare that followed the end

[33] *Adair v. United States*, 208 U.S. 161 (1908).
[34] *Hoke*, 227 U.S. at 323, quoted in *Caminetti v. United States*, 242 U.S. 470, 492 (1917).
[35] *Coppage v. Kansas*, 236 U.S. 1 (1915); *Adkins v. Children's Hospital*, 261 U.S. 525 (1823).

of World War I, the attorney general of the United States created an anti-radical division within the Department of Justice. Between 1919 and 1920, that division ordered a series of raids, known as Palmer raids after the attorney general who coordinated them, of organizations suspected of radical or subversive tendencies. These raids, which typically were conducted without warrants, often resulted in the arrest of quite a few people, who were often held without being charged, denied access to legal counsel, and frequently deported if they were not U.S. citizens.

CONCLUSION

At the start of the twentieth century, efforts to bring popular justice under control and subordinate it to the power of the State took a variety of forms. Some of the approaches looked familiar. Governments continued to try to professionalize the police and reform the courts, especially the petty courts that dealt with the vast majority of the criminal defendants. Reformers pushed for changes in the laws defining crimes, procedures for investigating and judging criminal acts, and processes for punishing those found guilty. Other factors continued to destabilize the efforts of the State to control criminal justice. Plea bargains became increasingly common, and sentences imposed through those private agreements often had little to do with the schemes of punishment worked out in statutes. The jockeying for power between state and federal governments continued, limiting the ability of either to gain a full monopoly on criminal justice. And extralegal forces, sometimes expressed through violence, other times through more peaceful forms of resistance, continued, weakening the power of the State as well.

6

RIGHTS AND THE TURN TO LAW, 1937–1939

Advocates of the rule of law had triumphed over proponents of lynching, but in other respects the constitutional order appeared to have broken down by the mid-1930s. Although the Supreme Court had taken steps to check mobs' ability to control the criminal courts, those decisions applied to only the most extreme cases. The rest of the time, due process, although valued – at least in the abstract – in the federal courts, was hardly a guarantee in state court criminal trials. Police departments, though stronger and marginally more professional than in the past, remained susceptible to corruption and public pressure and far too inclined to abuse their power. The forces of popular justice were often prejudiced against outsiders and easily manipulated. But then, in 1937, the Supreme Court suggested that it was willing to shift the constitutional order to bring those problems under control. Taking a leaf from the efforts to eradicate lynching, the Court approved congressional efforts to move disputes out of the streets and into the courts. At the same time, it altered its own view of rights, suggesting the possibility that it would be more receptive to efforts by state court criminal defendants and outsiders to use claims of rights.

FAILURE

The summer of 1937 revealed the extent of the breakdown.[1] In May 1937, the Steelworkers Organizing Committee (SWOC) went on strike against several steel companies, including Republic Steel, to compel them to recognize the union and negotiate a contract. By month's end the strike had closed thirty-seven plants and between 70,000 and 85,000 workers were off the job. On Memorial Day, 1937, more than a thousand people – men, women, and children – marched across an empty field toward the Republic Steel plant on Chicago's far south side. The purpose of the march was to protest Republic's refusal, in violation of state law, to allow striking steelworkers to picket peacefully outside the plant. Less than ten yards from the gate of the plant, the marchers came face to face with a wall of several hundred armed Chicago police officers, a line backed by an unknown number of company police and other men inside Republic's fence. It is unclear precisely what happened next. Paramount Pictures was filming the march for its newsreel program, but right at the point when the marchers met the police the cameraman paused to change his lens. By the time he began filming again, shots had been fired by the police and the marchers were retreating, some throwing stones at the police officers as they went. The next several minutes of film recorded more shots fired by the police, more marchers throwing rocks, and police officers advancing on fallen marchers to beat them with clubs. The entire incident lasted less than half an hour; when it was over six marchers lay dead and four more were mortally wounded. Thirty other marchers (including a number of women and children) had sustained gunshot

[1] Donald Gene Sofchalk, "The Little Steel Strike of 1937" (Ph.D. diss., Ohio State University, 1961).

wounds and nine were permanently disabled. Another twenty-eight marchers were hospitalized for other sorts of injuries, including a significant number of head wounds caused by police nightsticks. Sixteen of the police officers were injured; none had a gunshot wound.

The legal response was swift and laughably one sided. More than fifty marchers were arrested and charged with conspiracy to commit an illegal act, and the state's attorney threatened to add conspiracy to commit murder charges against some of the defendants. A coroner's inquest was called; when it finally met in July, the coroner's jury concluded that all the deaths during the Memorial Day march were justifiable. A grand jury was impaneled, but indicted no one. Those legal maneuvers took place against a steady beat from the Chicago press, which, led by the *Chicago Tribune*, praised the police for their actions during the march and declared that they had prevented a revolution. Not everyone agreed, of course; those attending a series of indignation meetings condemned Republic Steel and the Chicago police. On June 8, at a mass meeting at the Chicago Opera House, a resolution was passed that denounced the events of Memorial Day as a "breakdown of [the] democratic process." A second resolution passed at the meeting called for a federal investigation into the connection between the Chicago police department and Republic Steel. But neither the resolutions nor the meetings had an effect. Instead, the Chicago police department and the state's attorney's office pursued their investigations with the single goal of trying to justify the actions of the police. They gathered affidavits that stated that the marchers carried sawed-off shotguns and a variety of other weapons, and declared that they had additional evidence that the march was instigated by Communists and outside agitators.

Other, independent investigations quickly disproved those claims. The first, by the muckraker Paul Anderson, was published in the *St. Louis Post-Dispatch*.[2] His stories cast the event as a police riot and demonstrated that the marchers had resorted to violence in self-defense when they were attacked by the police wielding tear gas, night-sticks, and guns. A subsequent investigation by the Senate Committee on Education and Labor confirmed that the police, prompted by pressure from the leaders of Republic Steel, precipitated the violence during the Memorial Day march.[3] In December 1937, the case came to an end with a whimper. Fifty marchers appeared in court and pleaded guilty to unlawful assembly. They were fined a dollar a piece. Several others, who were from out of town, pleaded guilty to the same charge and were fined ten dollars. No one from Republic Steel or the police department was charged; no one was ever prosecuted for the deaths dur-ing the march. In a series of rulings issued between 1938 and 1941, the National Labor Relations Board resolved the issues underlying the strike, ruling that Republic Steel and the other companies had engaged in a series of unfair labor practices over the course of the strike. The Board ordered the companies to recognize and negotiate with the steelworkers union.[4]

The Memorial Day Massacre, as the event came to be called, was not the only violent incident during the steel strike that summer. Things got off to a bloody start on the strike's second day when a guard at one of Republic's plants in Canton, Ohio, shot a factory foreman after mis-taking him for a worker. When Republic tried to airlift

---

[2] *St. Louis Post-Dispatch*, June 16, 1937, 1–2; *St. Louis Post-Dispatch*, June 17, 1937, 1, 3; *St. Louis Post-Dispatch*, June 20, 1937, 1, 30.

[3] United States Senate, *Report of the Committee on Education and Labor: Part IV, The Little Steel Strike and Citizens Committees* (1941).

[4] *Republic Steel and SWOC*, 9 NLRB 219 (1938); *Inland Steel and SWOC*, 9 NLRB 783 (1938); *Bethlehem Steel and SWOC*, 14 NLRB 539 (1939); *Youngstown Steel & Tube and SWOC*, 31 NLRB 338 (1941).

food to guards and workers inside a plant in Warren, Ohio, striking workers on the ground allegedly shot at the plane, and guards retaliated by firing at the workers. Six workers were killed in strike-related incidents in Ohio, and countless others were injured in Ohio and Pennsylvania. The violence was predictable. Republic and the other steel companies created and often armed "citizens' committees," essentially vigilante groups, to put community pressure on striking workers and government officials in various steel towns around the country. They also helped supply local police and governments with ammunition, just in case. As the events in Chicago demonstrated, local government officials did their bit to help. The mayor of Johnston, Pennsylvania, for example, deputized vigilantes from the local American Legion post in June 1937 and armed them so that they could help put down the strike. The strikers were not nearly as well armed, so SWOC tried to put public pressure on local businesses and government agencies using a combination of social pressure and threats of violence, but local businesses tended to support the steel companies. In the end, the steel companies were able to break the strike, in large part because of their use of extralegal methods and their ability to hide those efforts behind the claim that a citizens' group, composed of local business leaders, represented popular hostility to the striking workers' goals.

Both sides of the Memorial Day Massacre claimed the power to take the law into their own hands to enforce their own notion of economic and social justice. It was, by 1937, a well-established pattern, as one professor of industrial relations made clear in comments published after the strike was broken.[5] He argued that the strike's

---

[5] "CIO Is Doomed as Un-American, Says Professor," *Chicago Tribune*, July 8, 1937, 11.

collapse revealed that the steelworkers' working-class ideology had been rejected as un-American and pointed, as
proof, to the evidence of popular opposition to the strike
in the form of citizens' associations, vigilante groups, and
other extralegal activities. The claim, mistaken as the subsequent investigation by the Senate Education and Labor
Committee revealed it to be, made two important points
about popular justice at the end of the 1930s: it was increasingly justified as the way to "protect" a community from
the threat posed by outsiders, with the result that claims
of the legitimacy of the extralegal activity turned on proving that the claimant was most entitled to use extralegal
powers. While those claims contained the echo of the older
arguments that the power to take the law into their own
hands belonged to the sovereign people, their emphasis
on difference and exclusion also echoed the hierarchy of
citizenship suggested by cases like *Dred Scott* and *Minor
v. Happersett.* Of course, that too was a familiar element
of extralegal justice, which long turned on dividing "us"
from "them" and justified attacks on "outsiders."

But the federal investigations into the steel strike of 1937
revealed another, newer element of extralegal justice. The
views of the professor of industrial relations notwithstanding, the violent disputes in Illinois, Ohio, and Pennsylvania
were not local or popular disagreements; they were nation-
ally organized battles fought on local turf. They were the
acts of mobs that had been manipulated by elites, not
spontaneous expressions of the will of an engaged sovereign people. Again, that was not entirely new. The lynch
mob that hanged Leo Frank had been egged on by elites
in Marietta, and contemporaries like George Templeton
Strong recognized (and rejoiced in the fact) that the vigilantes in San Francisco had been roused to act by local
business leaders. But those were local elites, whose ties to
the community gave them some incentive, at least in theory,

to control the violence and anger they unleashed. The steel strike of 1937 suggested that nationwide corporations, and nationwide unions, were not subject to similar constraints. It also raised the question of whether the state governments could be counted on to respond and suggested that they would, instead, allow themselves to be co-opted.

LEGALISM AND THE TURN TO RIGHTS

Congress and the Supreme Court had long shown themselves to be tolerant of local extralegal violence; cynics might add that both accepted extralegal violence that separated "us" from "them," since both had frequently approved or enabled legal practices that drew similar distinctions. But in 1937, the Court suggested that it was not willing to tolerate extralegal justice on a national scale, at least when it posed a threat to the nation's economy.

The process of pushing back against national extralegal justice began earlier; it was one of the justifications for the injunction against the railroad workers that the Court upheld in *In re Debs*. But in the 1920s and 1930s, Congress had begun to explore the idea that business was as much a threat as labor. And in 1935 Congress made that point even stronger when it passed the Wagner Act.[6] In the preamble to that Act, Congress blamed management far more than labor, for the strikes and violence that had burdened commerce and disrupted the economy, and declared: "Experience has proved that protection by law of the right of employees to organize and bargain collectively safeguards commerce from injury ... and promotes the flow of commerce by removing certain recognized sources of industrial strife and unrest, by encouraging practices fundamental to the friendly adjustment of industrial

---

[6] 49 Stat. 449 (1935).

disputes arising out of differences as to wages, hours, or other working conditions, and by restoring equality of bargaining power between employers and employees."

Congress's promise that the Wagner Act would end violence in the streets by turning disputes over economic justice into claims for rights and moving the disputes into the legal system set the groundwork for the reforms of 1937. That year the Supreme Court endorsed both the turn to law and the embrace of rights. The Court took the first move in *West Coast Hotel v. Parish*, decided in March 1937.[7] There the Supreme Court upheld a state law that made it illegal for businesses to refuse to pay women a minimum wage. In the process, the Court rejected the principle, set out in *Lochner v. New York* and other cases, that business and labor negotiated from positions of equality; instead it echoed Congress's conclusion that the two groups were not equal and that, as a result, workers required special legal protections and rights.

The next month, the Court decided *Jones & Laughlin v. NLRB*.[8] In that decision, the Court declared that the Wagner Act was constitutional. Two years later, the Court made explicit its commitment to the idea that legal remedies were preferable to extralegal actions in *NLRB v. Fansteel*. There, the Court held that sit-down strikes, where workers occupied a factory and refused to leave until their demands were resolved, were not protected by the Wagner Act. As the Court put it, "There is not a line in the statute to warrant the conclusion that it is any part of the policies of the Act to encourage employees to resort to force and violence in defiance of the law of the land. On the contrary, the purpose of the Act is to promote peaceful settlements of disputes by providing legal remedies for the invasion

---

[7] 300 U.S. 379 (1937).
[8] 301 U.S. 1 (1937).

of the employees' rights."⁹ The point was clear: extralegal acts, even those that were not injurious or violent, were no longer acceptable ways to resolve disagreements over what justice required. Disputes had to be moved off the streets and into the legal system, where they could be peaceably resolved.

A third case, decided at the very end of 1937, suggested the nature of the new constitutional order that the Court envisioned and began to explain the place of rights in that order. The case was *Palko v. Connecticut,* where the Court refused to conclude that the double jeopardy clause of the Fifth Amendment was incorporated into the Fourteenth Amendment.¹⁰ While that result seemed to reflect the Court's long-standing rejection of incorporation in criminal trials, the decision in *Palko* set out a new standard for deciding whether a right should be incorporated. The old standard, set out in *Hurtado,* hinged on the question of whether the right in question appeared to be a fundamental part of Anglo-American jurisprudence.¹¹ That put the emphasis on the historic nature of trials. In contrast, the new standard asked whether the right protected by a particular amendment was "the very essence of a scheme of ordered liberty," which put the emphasis both on the present and on social order.¹² Consistent with that emphasis, in *Palko* the Court suggested that there was a hierarchy of rights, with the First Amendment and its protections of liberty of expression and conscience taking pride of place. That not only tied rights to society rather than the courts, but also reflected the Court's recent emphasis on discussion and the peaceful airing of disagreement.

---

⁹ *NLRB v. Fansteel,* 306 U.S. 240, 258 (1939).
¹⁰ *Palko,* 302 U.S. 319 (1937). The Court later reversed that ruling in *Benton v. Maryland,* 395 U.S. 784 (1969).
¹¹ *Hurtado,* 110 U.S. at 536.
¹² 302 U.S. at 215.

The next year, in *United States v. Carolene Products,* the Court explained its judgment in *Parish* and suggested a willingness to move beyond the narrow framing in *Palko.*[13] *Carolene Products* was a regulatory crime case; the defendant was charged and had been found guilty of selling adulterated milk in interstate commerce, in violation of the Filled Milk Act (1924). The Court affirmed the defendant's conviction, upholding the Act as a legitimate exercise of congressional power under the commerce clause. The Court also rejected the argument that the law was unconstitutional because it was an exercise of police power, which was a power exclusively granted to the states.[14] In that respect, the opinion did no more than earlier decisions had done. But if *Carolene Products* recognized that various parts of the Constitution gave Congress police powers, which, in turn, allowed Congress to enact laws that criminalized conduct and to provide punishments for those crimes, it also went beyond affirming that the state and federal governments shared police power and the ability to legislate in the area of criminal law. In footnote 4 of its opinion, the Court explained its decision in *West Coast Hotel v. Parish,* declaring that it would no longer presume that laws that restricted or regulated economic rights (like liberty of contract) were unconstitutional. Instead, it would henceforth subject such laws to a rational basis test. That meant that "the existence of facts supporting the legislative judgment is to be presumed, … unless, in the light of the facts made known or generally assumed, it is of such a character as to preclude the assumption that it rests upon some rational basis within the knowledge and experience of the legislators." In that

---

[13] *United States v. Carolene Products,* 304 U.S. 144 (1938).
[14] 304 U.S. at 147.

footnote, the Court also noted that it would henceforth apply a different standard in evaluating a statute that "appears on its face to be within a specific prohibition of the Constitution, such as those of the first ten amendments, which are deemed equally specific when held to be embraced within the Fourteenth," or that appeared to be designed to restrict political processes, or that targeted "discrete and insular minorities." Statutes that fell into those categories would be subject to strict scrutiny and presumed to be unconstitutional.

Rights, in that view, were no longer a means of distinguishing categories of citizens. Instead, they had been redefined as a means of ensuring the peaceful airing and resolution of difference. And in concert with the new emphasis on the courts, they had provided a way to end practices, legal or extralegal, that tried to divide communities into "us" and "them."

FROM SOVEREIGNS TO SUBJECTS?

In their different opinions in *Hurtado v. California* (1884), Justices Matthews and Harlan set out the two sides of criminal justice between 1789 and 1939. For Justice Matthews, writing for the majority, the courts, judges, and laws were in place to protect those accused of crimes and the community in which they lived. Those institutes of the State, working through the rule of law, would make sure that accusations brought through error or bias would not result in unjust convictions, but would also guarantee that those who had committed crimes would be punished and the community's interest in peace preserved. As he put it, "The enforcement of these limitations by judicial process is the device of self-governing communities to protect the rights of individuals and minorities, as well against the power of numbers as against the violence of public agents transcending the limits of lawful authority, even when acting in the name and wielding the force of the government."[15]

Writing in dissent, Justice Harlan denied that the structures and agents of the State could be trusted to that extent. Noting that in many states judges were elected and therefore highly responsive to both the will and the prejudices of the voters, Harlan argued that the law and its power could too easily be abused and could not be allowed to function without some sort of independent check. The grand jury, he added, fulfilled precisely that role while also checking popular prejudice: "In the secrecy of the investigations by grand juries, the weak and helpless – proscribed, perhaps, because of their race, or pursued by an unreasoning public clamor – have found, and will continue to find, security against official oppression, the cruelty of mobs, the machinations of falsehood, and the malevolence of private persons who would use the machinery of the law to bring ruin upon their personal enemies."[16]

Their disagreements captured the fundamental tensions in criminal justice in the first 150 years of the constitutional era. How were the power of the government and the power of the people to be balanced? How could the community be protected from harm, with the assurance that neither the government nor the public could abuse the law to unjustly or unfairly punish people for crimes? By 1937 the Supreme Court had concluded that the answer was to move beyond the solutions the two justices offered, looking past the protections provided by due process and the rule of law or the check offered by the secrecy of the independent, popularly based grand jury. Instead, the Court opened the door to the very idea that *Hurtado* had rejected, allowing the standards

[15]   110 U.S. at 536.
[16]   110 U.S. at 544–555.

of the U.S. Constitution and the Bill of Rights to serve as a measure against which processes of criminal justice could be checked. And to make it more likely that would work, the Court endorsed congressional efforts to push disputes out of the streets and into the courts. That was a new view of rights. In the nineteenth century, rights had provided a means of drawing distinctions between citizens; by the late 1930s, rights had become a means for all people to check the power of the State. This view reflected the shift away from popular sovereignty to a model that used legal institutions and balances of rights and interests to diffuse differences and resolve disputes. And it rested on the sense, supported by considerable evidence, that for too long popular justice, either inside or outside the courts, had been too responsive to prejudice or "unreasoning public clamor." But questions about what that meant remained. Could the turn to rights result in all those things, or would it simply reinforce divisions within society as they had before? Would the new regime of rights hamper the institutions of criminal justice to the extent that disorder would prevail or help check abuses of governmental power? Would it separate law even more from justice or help reconcile the two?

In 1939 there were several ways to think about the shift. The Court and Congress suggested that the shift reflected a new commitment to the ideal of equal justice, reinforced by a renewed commitment to the rule of law and less violence. In that view, community-based justice was always too inclined to favor the known over the unknown, too prone to find the marginal and the minority guilty of crimes and to excuse the abuses and injuries caused by or called for by the majority. Shifting from a regime of popular justice to the rule of law would, in this view, protect those outside the community and the community itself from violence, while the turn toward rights would protect the sovereign people's interest in controlling government.

According to that theory, rights were a means by which the sovereign people could maintain their sovereign power in a more peaceful fashion. But it was also possible to read the rise of rights as proof that Alexander Hamilton had been correct. Writing in *The Federalist*, Hamilton had famously argued that there was no need to add a Bill of Rights to the U.S. Constitution, because "Bills of Rights are in their origin, stipulations between kings and their subjects, abridgements of prerogative in favor of privileges, reservations of rights not surrendered to the king."[17] The ideas of popular or rough justice had often rested, and had typically been excused, on the basis of the theory that the people could and should take the law into their own hands because they were sovereign. Did submission to a regime of legal remedies and an embrace of the idea of rights mean the people had sacrificed their claim to sovereign power? Or was the truth somewhere in between? Not at the comforting middle space between two extremes, but at a spot that was subjected to perpetual contest? A spot that was constantly subject to the struggles between the active citizenry intent on preserving and engaging its sovereign powers, governments that were equally intent on maintaining control, and local and national enterprises that tried to manipulate those disputes to advance their own, typically economic ends? On paper, the constitutional order seemed much changed, but the issue of whether those changes would take effect and significantly alter criminal justice in the United States awaited another day.

[17] Publius [Alexander Hamilton], *The Federalist*, No. 84.

CONCLUSION

And so the history of criminal justice during the first 150 years of the constitutional era is not really a simple story of the rise of the State. Instead, it is an account of how three sovereigns – national, local, and popular – struggled to determine who could define and enforce justice. In the United States between 1789 and 1939, that history of criminal justice unfolded on four levels. At its most basic, it was a story of the changes and continuities revealed by comparing the Nettles and Cannon case at the beginning of the nineteenth century with the trial of McAllister a century later. Observers of one era would have understood the processes and recognized the participants of the other, yet they would have also noticed the significant differences of emphasis (the greater focus on the logic of law in the later period), of institutions (the role of the police and the medical examiner), and of evidence (the new approaches to expert witnesses).

At the same time, the history of criminal justice is a story of a struggle for sovereign power between the state and federal governments. That struggle began with a default, as Congress failed to act in the realm of criminal law at the beginning of the constitutional era, and ended with two assertions of federal authority, when the Supreme Court declared that it would permit far greater oversight of state court processes and Congress began to create the administrative state that would wrest power from state governments. Significant as those changes were, that second layer of history was shaped by interaction with a third, in which the institutions of formal law, state or national, intersected with the forces of popular justice. Over time those popular forces and their relation to the criminal justice system changed. Sometimes the people were part of criminal justice, and sometimes they acted in competition with it, but whatever their role they shaped the responses of both state and federal government and helped direct the changes in criminal justice over time. The final layer of this history ties those different segments together, tracing the connections between the changes in the system of criminal justice and the shifts in constitutional order between 1789 and 1939.

BIBLIOGRAPHIC ESSAY

Although it builds on other histories of criminal justice in the United States, this study approaches that subject from a very different perspective. Most histories of criminal law are based on the Weberian thesis that associates modernity with the State's acquisition of a monopoly on violence (Max Weber, "Politics as Vocation," *The Theory of Social and Economic Organization* [1947, 1968], 154; Andreas Kalyvas, *Democracy and the Politics of the Extraordinary: Max Weber, Carl Schmitt, and Hannah Arendt* [2008]), which is demonstrated by the centralization of criminal justice. See Doreen J. McBarnet, *Criminal Law: The State and the Construction of Justice* (1981).

In contrast, this study is influenced by scholarship that calls that story into question. Its starting point is Charles Tilly's idea that extralegal activity like banditry exists along the same continuum as policing; see Tilly, "War Making and State Making as Organized Crime," in Peter B. Evans, Dietrech Rueschemeyer, and Theda Skocpol, eds., *Bringing the State Back In* (1985), 169, 170. It also builds on other works that have explored how people and forces outside the formal system of law judge and punish behavior. See, for example, Marcus Rediker, *Between the Devil and the Deep Blue Sea: Merchant Sailors, Pirates, 1700–1760* (1987) (judging and punishing aboard ship); Walter O. Weyrauch, "Unwritten Constitutions, Unwritten Law," *Washington & Lee Law Review* 56 (1999): 1211 (informal legal systems created by communities and groups). It also stems from other works of U.S. history that assert that the authority of the rule of law was contested throughout the nineteenth century. See Christopher Tomlins, *Law, Labor and Ideology in the Early American Republic* (1989) (tracing the significance of the police as an alternative to the rule of law in the first half of the nineteenth century); Elizabeth Dale, *The Rule of Justice: The People of Chicago versus Zephyr Davis* (2001) (arguing that even at the end of the nineteenth century the rule of justice was often subordinated to popular notions of justice). Others demonstrate that for much of the nineteenth century the very idea of the State was challenged by notions of popular sovereignty. See, for example, Larry Kramer, *The People Themselves: Popular Constitutionalism and Judicial Review* (2004) (popular constitutionalism across the United States through the 1830s); Christian G. Fritz, *American Sovereigns: The People and American's Constitutional Tradition before the Civil War* (2007) (the strength of popular sovereignty before 1860); Philip Ethington, *The Public City: The Political Construction of Urban Life in San Francisco, 1850–1900* (2001) (popular challenges to state power in California during the vigilante era in the second half of the nineteenth century); Stephen Kantrowitz, *Ben Tillman and the Reconstruction of White Supremacy* (2000) (the claims of popular [white] authority to act in place of the courts in late-nineteenth-century South Carolina); Mary Ryan, *Civic Wars: Democracy and Public Life in the American City During the Nineteenth Century* (1998) (describing the powers of popular forces over government throughout the nineteenth century).

These studies suggest a complex taxonomy of law and justice. They reveal that popular forces sometimes functioned as an alternative to formal law or in its absence (Tomlins, *Law, Labor and Ideology*; Ethington, *Public City*) and at other times competed with formal law and legal institutions (Kramer, *People Themselves*; Ryan, *Civic Wars*), and on still other occasions complemented and reinforced the institutions of the State and formal legal processes (William Novak, "The Myth of the 'Weak' American State," *American Historical Review* 113 [2008]: 752 [describing a local State often composed of private organizations exercising State-like functions]). Taken together, these studies reveal the strength of non-State forces for much of the long nineteenth century, raising questions of the limits and alternatives to State power that this essay touches upon and that studies of criminal law should consider in greater detail in years to come.

General Sources for the History of Criminal Law in the United States, 1789–1939

National Studies

The historiography of criminal law can be neatly divided into three types: national surveys, regional studies, and local sources. There are two major histories of criminal law in the United States; each devotes a considerable amount of space to examining the nature of criminal law in the nineteenth century: Samuel Walker, *Popular Justice: A History of American Criminal Justice* (2d ed., 1998); Lawrence M. Friedman, *Crime and Punishment in American History* (1993). In addition, overviews of American legal history devote space to criminal law in the period covered by this essay: Lawrence M. Friedman, *American Law in the*

Twentieth Century (2002); Kermit Hall, *The Magic Mirror: Law in American History* (1989); Lawrence M. Friedman, *A History of American Law* (2d ed., 1985). Most histories of criminal law in the United States tie developments in the criminal justice system to the rise of the local State after the founding era. See, for example, Walker, *Popular Justice*; Friedman, *Crime and Punishment*; Allan Steinberg, *The Transformation of Criminal Justice: Philadelphia, 1800–1880* (1989); Kermit Hall, *The Magic Mirror: Law in American History* (1989). Those studies are part of a larger literature that debates the existence and location of the nineteenth-century American State. The *Cambridge History of Law in America* includes several chapters that sketch the scope of this debate: Mark R. Wilson, "Law and the American State, from the Revolution to the Civil War: Institutional Growth and Structural Change," *Cambridge History*, Vol. 2: 1 (2008); William E. Forbath, "Politics, State-Building and the Courts," *Cambridge History*, Vol. 2: 643; Daniel R. Ernst, "Law and the State, 1920–2000: Institutional Growth and Structural Change," *Cambridge History*, Vol. 3: 1 (2008). Recently, several other studies have suggested that the American State was created by public–private partnerships during the nineteenth century. See, for example, Brian Balogh, *A Government Out of Sight: The Mystery of National Authority in Nineteenth-Century America* (2009) (arguing that there was a nation-state during the long nineteenth century and that that state acted mostly to facilitate private development through infrastructure).

Studies that tie American criminal justice to the rise of the local State are reinforced by scholarship that describes the creation of a distinctively American legal system designed to mix social control and market capitalism. See, for example, Charles Sellers, *The Market Revolution: Jacksonian American, 1815–1846* (1991); Morton J. Horwitz, *The*

Transformation of American Law, 1780–1860 (1977); William E. Nelson, *The Americanization of the Common Law: The Impact of Legal Change on American Law, 1760–1830* (1975). When they link the rise of the State to criminal law, histories of the nineteenth century assume the rule of law, noting its absence as an anomaly particular to a region or culture. See, for example, Michael Hindus, *Prison and Plantation: Crime, Justice and Authority in Massachusetts and South Carolina, 1767–1878* (1980); Edward Ayers, *Vengeance and Justice: Crime and Punishment in the Nineteenth-Century American South* (1984). In this respect as well, histories of criminal law are not much different from American legal histories, which typically date the establishment of the rule of law to the writing of the Constitution, if not before. Consider, for example, John Phillip Reid, *Rule of Law: The Jurisprudence of Liberty in the Seventeenth and Eighteenth Centuries* (2004). While most studies of the history of criminal law in the United States focus exclusively on that country, several recent studies consider the history of criminal justice in the United States in comparison with criminal justice systems in other countries. See, for example, Dario Melossi, *Controlling Crime, Controlling Society: Thinking About Crime in Europe and America* (2008); Daniel Siemens, *Metropole and Verbrechen: Die Gerichts reportage in Berlin, Paris, and Chicago, 1919–1933* (2009).

Regionalism and State-Specific Studies

For most of the nation's history (and throughout the nineteenth century) criminal law was a local matter, and not unexpectedly many studies have argued that regional differences led to regionally distinctive systems of criminal law. This theory has had its greatest hold with respect to the South. In 1940 Charles S. Sydnor argued that a combination of economic, religious, and cultural characteristics made the legal culture of the antebellum South distinctive; see Sydnor, "The Southerner and the Laws," *Journal of Southern History* 6 (1940): 3. In the years since, historians have offered variations on that theme. See, for example, Christopher Waldrep, *Roots of Disorder: Race and Criminal Justice in the American South, 1817–1880* (1998) (race relations create a distinctive legal culture); Peter Bardaglio, *Reconstructing the Household: Families, Sex and the Law in the Nineteenth-Century South* (1995) (a combination of honor culture and gender norms created a unique southern legal system until the late antebellum era, when economic shifts brought the legal system more in line with that of the North); Ayers, *Vengeance and Justice* (religion and honor culture create a unique system of justice); Bertram Wyatt-Brown, *Southern Honor: Ethics and Behavior in the Old South* (1982) (patriarchy and honor culture create a specifically southern system of law). However, some recent histories have challenged the idea of southern distinctiveness, arguing that criminal law in the South tracked shifts in law across the country: Laura Edwards, *The People and Their Peace: Legal Culture and the Transformation of Inequality in the Post-Revolutionary South* (2009) (making this point for the first half of the nineteenth century); Michael Pfeifer, *Rough Justice: Lynching and American Society, 1874–1947* (2004) (making the point with respect to the late nineteenth and early twentieth centuries).

Histories of the western United States have tried to challenge the idea that the West was a uniquely lawless frontier. See Clare V. McKanna, Jr., *Race and Homicide in Nineteenth-Century California* (2002); John Phillip Reid, *Protecting the Elephant: Property and Social Behavior on the Overland Trail* (reprint ed., 1997), Robert D. McGrath, *Gunfighters, Highwaymen, and Vigilantes: Violence on the Frontier* (1984); Robert R. Dykstra, "Quantifying the Wild West: The Problematic Statistics of Frontier Violence," *Western Historical Quarterly* 40 (2009): 321. Interestingly, although he challenges the idea that the South had a distinctive criminal justice system in the late nineteenth and early twentieth centuries, Michael Pfeifer's recent study of rough justice suggests that criminal justice in the New England states was different in that period.

In addition to the regional studies, there are a number of studies that look at criminal law in particular states or cities during some or all of the nineteenth century. Examples are Jeffrey Adler, *First in Violence, Deepest in Dirt: Homicide in Chicago, 1875–1920* (2006); Eric Monkkonen, *Murder in New York City* (2000); Roger Lane, *Violent Death in the City: Suicide, Accident and Murder in Nineteenth-Century Philadelphia* (2d ed., 1999); Allen Steinberg, *The Transformation of Criminal Law: Philadelphia, 1800–1880* (1989); Lawrence M. Friedman and Robert V. Perceival, *The Roots of Justice: Crime and Punishment in Alameda County, California, 1870–1910* (1981); Michael Hindus, *Prison and Plantation: Criminal Justice and Authority in Massachusetts and South Carolina* (1980) (which is, as its title suggests, a comparative work); Jack Kenny Williams, *Vogues in Villainy: Crime and Retribution in Ante-bellum South Carolina* (1959). Some of these studies, such as Williams, *Vogues in Villainy*, reinforce the idea of regional distinctiveness; others, such as Lane, *Violent Death in the City*, and Monkkonen, *Murder in New York*, both of which found honor culture in northern cities, seem to undermine it.

Police and Policing

Police departments were first established, and then significantly reformed, during the course of the nineteenth century. As a result there are a number of studies of police forces in the nineteenth century: Sally Hadden, *Slave Patrols: Law and Violence in Virginia and the Carolinas* (2000) (comparing the policing of slaves in several southern states); Wilbur R. Miller, *Cops and Bobbies: Police Authority in New York and London, 1830–1870* (2d ed., 1999); Richard C. Lindberg, *To Serve and Collect: Chicago Politics and Police Corruption from the Lager Beer Riot the Summerdale Scandal, 1855–1960* (1998); Dennis C. Rousey, *Policing the Southern City: New Orleans, 1805–1889* (1996) (generally about New Orleans, although the book discusses policing in other southern cities); Eric H. Monkkonen, *Police in Urban America, 1860–1920* (1981), David R. Johnson, *American Law Enforcement: A History* (1981); Roger Lane, *Policing the City: Boston, 1882–1885* (1971), Sam Bass Warner, Jr., *The Private City: Philadelphia in Three Periods of Its Growth* (1968) (policing in Philadelphia during the antebellum era in ch. 7); Roger D. McGrath, "A Violent Birth: Disorder, Crime and Law Enforcement, 1849–1890," *California History* 81 (2003): 27. The rise of police record keeping is described in Saran Ghatak, "'The Whole Extent of the Evil': Origins of Crime Statistics in the United States, 1880–1930," *Journal of Historical Statistics* 21 (2008): 30.

Because of the nature of police work, the subject of policing also comes up in urban histories, labor histories, and studies of immigration and race relations. There are, for example, glimpses of the reorganization of the Chicago police department in the late nineteenth century in Richard Schneirov, *Labor and Urban Politics: Class Conflict and the Origins of Modern Liberalism in Chicago, 1864–1897* (1998), and discussions of the first African American officers on Chicago's police force in *Black Chicago's First Century: Volume 1, 1833–1900* (2005). But more could be done to explore the integration of blacks, immigrants, and women into police forces. Women were hired to serve on

some police forces in the late nineteenth and early twentieth centuries. See Mary Jane Aldrich-Moodie, "Staking
Out Their Domain: Women in the New York City Police
Department, 1890–1935" (Ph.D. diss., University of North
Carolina, 2002); Doris Schargenberg, "The Division Has
Become a Necessity," *Michigan History Magazine* 86
(2002): 76 (women in the Detroit police department, beginning in 1920); Samuel Walker, "The Rise and Fall of the
Police Women's Movement, 1905–1975," *Law and Order
in American History* (1979): 101. However, there are few
studies that explore their experiences or their impact.

Given the significant role the police play in the criminal
justice system, more could be done to explore nineteenth-
century policing at the local level. At the same time, the
studies by Miller, Rousey, and Hadden suggest the value of
considering policing in a comparative context. An essay by
Clive Emsley, which reviews the literature on nineteenth-
century policing in several European countries (notably
England, France, Italy, and Prussia), sets out a typology
of policing that might be fruitfully applied to future studies of police departments in the United States. See Clive
Emsley, "A Typology of Nineteenth-Century Police,"
Crime, Histoire & Sociétés 3 (1999): 29.

Crimes

Murder

The nineteenth-century United States had higher murder
rates than countries in western Europe, and this fact has
preoccupied quite a few historians. Two studies, Randall
Roth, *Homicide in America* (2009), and Roger Lane,
Murder in America: A History (1997), examine homicide throughout the country, but most studies are more
narrowly focused. Many consider conviction rates in particular cities: Lane, *Violent Death in the City*; Monkkonen,

Murder in New York; Adler, *First in Violence, Deepest in Dirt*; Eric Monkkonen, "Homicide in Los Angeles, 1827–2002," *Journal of Interdisciplinary History* 36 (2005): 167. Others look at states or regions: William Lynwood Montell, *Killings: Folk Justice in the Upper South* (1986) (a county at the Kentucky–Tennessee border); Gilles Vandal, *Southern Violence: Homicides in Post-Civil War Louisiana, 1866–1884* (2000); Clare V. McKanna, Jr., *Race and Homicide in Nineteenth-Century California* (2002). A quick glance at these works reveals little agreement about why homicide rates in the nineteenth century were so high, although both Roth and Lane attempt to explain America's exceptionalism in their works. The debates over the reasons for the high homicide rate in the United States are set out in two forums: *American Historical Review*, 111 (2006): 75; and *Social Science History* 25 (2001): 1.

Morals Legislation

While there are a few exceptions – see, for example, Robert M. Ireland, "The Problem of Concealed Weapons in Nineteenth-Century Kentucky," *Register of the Kentucky Historical Society* 91 (1993): 370 – much of the work on crime in the nineteenth century has focused on what Lawrence M. Friedman called the "Victorian Compromise," the ambiguous relationship between stricter regulation of morality through criminal laws and actual enforcement of those laws; see Friedman, *Crime and Punishment*. Not surprisingly, many of these studies have focused on sex crimes and crimes arising from sexual relations. See, for example, Thomas C. Mackey, *Pursuing Johns: Criminal Law Reform, Defending Character, and New York City's Committee of Fourteen, 1920–1930* (2005); Don Ramesburg, "'Wouldn't a Boy Do?' Placing Early Twentieth Century Male Youth Sexuality into the History of Sexuality," *Journal of the History of Sexuality* 18 (2009): 367; Julie Novkov, "Racial

Constructions: The Legal Regulation of Miscegenation in Alabama, 1890–1934," *Law and History Review* 20 (2002): 225; Joel Best, *Controlling Vice: Regulating Brothel Prostitution in St. Paul, 1865–1883* (1998); Leslie J. Reagan, *When Abortion Was a Crime: Women, Medicine and Law in the United States, 1867–1973* (1997) (the criminalization of abortion); Timothy J. Gilfoyle, *City of Eros: New York City, Prostitution, and the Commercialization of Sex, 1790–1920* (1992) (the regulation of prostitution and prosecution of vice); Mary E. Odem, *Delinquent Daughters: Protecting and Policing Adolescent Female Sexuality in the United States, 1885–1920* (1995).

A number of works consider the rise of blue laws and temperance legislation in the nineteenth century: Peter Wallenstein, "Never on Sunday: Blue Laws and Roanoke, Virginia," *Virginia Cavalcade* 43 (1994): 132; Joseph B. Marks and Lisa J. Sanders, "The Blue Laws Debate: A Sacramento Shopkeeper's Story," *Western States Jewish History*, 25 (1993): 211; Raymond Schmandt, "The Pastor of Loretto, Pennsylvania, versus the All-American Game of Baseball," *Western Pennsylvania Historical Magazine*, 69 (1986): 81; Arnold Roth, "Sunday 'Blue Laws' and the California State Supreme Court," *Southern California Quarterly* 55 (1973): 43; Vernon Lestrud, "Early Theatrical 'Blue Laws' on the Pacific Coast," *Rendezvous* 4 (1969): 15 (blue laws in California, Oregon, and Washington); Maxine S. Seller, "Isaac Leeser: A Jewish–Christian Dialogue in Antebellum Philadelphia," *Pennsylvania History* 35 (1968): 231 (Leeser's activities against blue laws); Harold E. Cox, "'Daily Except Sunday': Blue Laws and the Operation of Philadelphia Horse Cars," *Business History Review* 39 (1965): 228; J. E. Ericson and James H. McCrocklin, "From Religion to Commerce: The Evolution and Enforcement of Blue Laws in Texas," *Southwestern Social Science Quarterly* 45 (1964): 50.

A third group of studies looks at efforts to pass temperance legislation: Ray Cunningham, "Virtue and Vice in Homer: The Battle for Morals in a Central Illinois Town, 1870–1890," *Illinois Heritage* 7 (2004): 14; Dale E. Soden, "The Women's Christian Temperance Union in the Pacific Northwest: The Battle for Cultural Control," *Pacific Northwest Quarterly*, 94 (2003): 197; Richard Hamm, *Shaping the Eighteenth Amendment: Temperance Reform, Legal Culture, and the Polity, 1880–1920* (1995); Donald Pitzer, "Revivalism and Politics in Toledo: 1899," *Northwest Ohio Quarterly* 41 (1968–1969): 13.

While most of these studies focus on state-level efforts to legislate morality, others trace the way that morals legislation became a federal issue: Gaines Foster, *Moral Reconstruction: Christian Lobbyists and the Federal Legislation of Morality, 1865–1920* (2002); Mara Keire, "The Vice Trust: A Reinterpretation of the White Slavery Scare in the United States, 1907–1917," *Journal of Social History* 35 (2001): 5; Hamm, *Shaping the Eighteenth Amendment*. Many of these books on morals legislation explore the role of reform networks, although more could be done to apply the insights of social movement literature, particularly *national* social movement literature, to the history of criminal law. Compare Michael P. Young, "Confessional Protest: The Religious Birth of United States' National Social Movements," *American Sociological Review* 67 (2002): 660 (examining antebellum temperance and anti-slavery movements as social movements on a national scale); Alan Hunt, *Governing Morals: A Social History of Moral Regulation* (1999). Several of the works in this area, most notably the studies by Foster and Young, suggest another aspect of criminal law that deserves more study, the significance of religion. While a few books, notably Susan Jacoby's *Wild Justice: The Evolution of Revenge* (1983), have argued that particular theological beliefs helped shape attitudes toward punishment, more could be done to examine the impact of religious ideas and religious groups on American theories of crime and punishment.

Studies of Other Crimes

A number of works look at rape and other crimes of intimacy, such as seduction, domestic violence, and sex practices. See, for example, Brian T. McCormick, "Conjugal Violence, Sex, Sin and Murder in the Mission Communities of Alta California," *Journal of History of Sexuality* 16 (2007): 391; Ruth Bloch, "The American Revolution, Wife Beating, and the Emergent Value of Privacy," *Early American Studies* 5 (2007): 223; Stephen Robertson, "'Boys, of Course, Cannot Be Raped': Age, Homosexuality, and the Redefinition of Sexual Violence in New York City, 1880–1950," *Gender and History* 18 (2006): 357; Stephen Roberts, "Seduction, Sexual Violence, and Marriage in New York City, 1886–1955," *Law & History Review* 24 (2006): 331. Still others look at crimes of fraud and confidence games (Stephen Mihm, *A Nation of Counterfeiters: Capitalists, Con Men and the Making of the United States* [2007]) and the related area of organized crime. For one recent study, see David Critchey, *The Origins of Organized Crime in America: The New York Mafia, 1891–1931* (2009).

Crime and People

Women and Crime

Some studies of women and crime look at crimes particularly related to women. See Joel Best, *Controlling Vice: Regulating Brothel Prostitution in St. Paul, 1865–1883* (1998); Reagan, *When Abortion Was a Crime*. Other studies look at women as criminals. See, for example, Susan Branson, *And Dangerous to Know: Women, Crime and*

Notoriety in the Early Republic (2008); Kali N. Gross, *Colored Amazons: Crime, Violence and Black Women in the City of Brotherly Love, 1880–1920* (2006); Best, *Controlling Vice*; Douglas V. Shaw, "Infanticide in New Jersey: A Nineteenth-Century Case Study," *New Jersey History* 115 (1997): 3. Some look at women as victims; McCormick, "Conjugal Violence, Sex, Sin"; Bloch, "The American Revolution, Wife Beating"; Sean T. Moore, "'Justifiable Provocation': Violence Against Women in Essex County, New York, 1799–1860," *Journal of Social History* 35 (2002): 889. And some examine women who were both criminals and victims: Odem, *Delinquent Daughters*; Best, *Controlling Vice*; Reagan, *When Abortion Was a Crime*.

Juveniles and Crime

The topic of youth and crime is dealt with in terms of the rise of the juvenile court system: Eric Schneider, *In the Web of Class: Delinquents and Reformers in Boston, 1810s–1930s* (1992). There are also studies that investigate the punishment of juveniles at the end of the nineteenth century: David Tanenhaus, *Juvenile Justice in the Making* (2004); David Wolcott, "Juvenile Justice Before Juvenile Courts: Cops, Courts and Kids in Turn-of-the-Century Detroit," *Social Science History* 27 (2003): 109; David Wolcott, "'The Cop Will Get You': The Police and Discretionary Juvenile Justice, 1890–1940," *Journal of Social History* 35 (2001): 319. It is also discussed in the context of alternatives to juvenile justice. See, for example, Janis Appers, "We're Blocking Youth's Path to Crime," *Journal of Women's History* 31 (2005): 190. Studies on other subjects also deal with the issue of youth offenders. See, for example, Robertson, "Boys, of Course, Cannot Be Raped"; Odem, *Delinquent Daughters*.

Slaves and Crime

A number of studies look at slaves and their experience of the criminal justice system. Edwards, *People and Their Peace*, considers the issue as part of her larger study of courts in the antebellum South. For studies concerned more precisely with slaves and the legal system in its various manifestations, see James Campbell, "'The Victim of Prejudice and Hasty Consideration': The Slave Trial System in Richmond Virginia, 1830–1861," *Slavery and Abolition* 26 (2005): 71; Philip J. Schwartz, *Twice Condemned Slaves and the Criminal Laws of Virginia, 1705–1865* (1988); William Cinque Henderson, "Spartan Slaves: A Documentary Account of Blacks on Trial in Spartanburg, South Carolina, 1830–1865" (Ph.D. diss., Northwestern University, 1978); Daniel Flannigan, "Criminal Procedure in Slave Trials in the Antebellum South," *Journal of Southern History* 40 (1974): 537; John C. Edwards, "Slave Justice in Four Middle Georgia Counties," *Georgia Historical Quarterly* 57 (1973): 265; Robert McPherson, ed., "Georgia Slave Trials, 1837–1841," *American Journal of Legal History* 4 (1960): 257; E. Merton Coulter, "Four Slave Trials in Elbert County, Georgia," *Georgia Historical Quarterly* 41 (1957): 237. For studies that analyze the sort of process that was considered due to slaves, see James Campbell, "'The Victim of Prejudice and Hasty Consideration': The Slave Trial System in Richmond, Virginia, 1930–1861," *Slavery & Abolition* 26 (2005): 71. For a study of slaves and criminal law in the context of a larger study of slaves and law, see Thomas D. Morris, *Southern Slavery and the Law, 1619–1860* (1999). Other studies look at how criminal law issues were translated to deal with the particular circumstances of slaves: Craig Bettinger, "Did Slaves Have Free Will? 'Luke, A Slave v. Florida' and Crimes at the Command of the Master," *Florida Historical*

Quarterly 83 (2005): 241; Glenn McNair, "Slave Women, Capital Crime, and the Criminal Justice System," *Georgia Historical Quarterly* 93 (2009): 135.

Immigrants, Racial and Ethnic Minorities, and Crime
In a 1974 essay, David Colburn and George Pozzetta called for studies exploring how minority groups experienced criminal justice in the United States; see their "Crime and Ethnic Minorities in America: A Bibliographic Essay," *History Teacher* 7 (1974): 597. A few studies, like Mary Tiing Yi Lui, *The Chinatown Trunk Mystery* (2005), examine the problem in the context of specific ethnic groups; see also Vanessa Gunther, "Indians and the Criminal Justice System in San Bernardino and San Diego Counties, 1850–1900," *Journal of the West* 39 (2000): 26.

Others look at the experiences of different groups in criminal justice systems: Adler, *First in Violence*; Phillip Chang Ho Shan and Anthony B. Chan, "Linking African American Ghettos and Chinatowns in 19th Century America: Implications for Criminological Theory," *Asian Profile* 38 (2010): 38. But surprisingly little has been done on specific problems immigrants faced in the criminal court system. In contrast, there has been more work examining African Americans' experience of the criminal justice system. See, for example, Gross, *Colored Amazons*; James B. Campbell, "'You Needn't Be Afraid Here, You're in a Civilized County': Region, Race, Violence and Law in Early Twentieth-Century New Jersey, New York, and Pennsylvania," *Social History* 35 (2010): 253; Patrick Lynn Rivers, "Race, Sex, Violence and the Problem of Agency in North Carolina, 1889–1903," *Australasian Journal of American Studies* 28 (2009): 34; Andrea Stone, "Interracial Sexual Abuse and Legal Subjectivity in Antebellum Law and Literature," *American Literature* 81 (2009): 65; Marcy Sacks, "To Show Who Was in Charge:

Police Repression of New York City's Black Population at the Turn of the Twentieth Century," *Journal of Urban History* 31 (2005): 799; Anne M. Butler, "Still in Chains: Black Women in Western Prisons, 1865–1910," *Western Historical Quarterly* 20 (1989): 18; Mary E. Seematter, "Trials and Confessions: Race and Justice in Antebellum St. Louis," *Gateway Heritage* 12 (1991): 36 (trial of four free blacks for murder and arson).

Procedures and Courts

Practice and Process

There are few histories that deal with criminal procedure or consider the roles of jurors, judges, or attorneys in criminal trials in the nineteenth century, and those that do so typically focus on individual states. Alan Rogers traced changes in criminal trials and procedure in Massachusetts in "Murder in Massachusetts: The Criminal Discovery Rule from *Snelling* to Rule 14," *Journal of American Legal History* 40 (1996): 438, and examined the history of court-appointed lawyers representing capital defendants in that state in "'A Sacred Duty': Court Appointed Attorneys in Massachusetts Capital Cases, 1780–1980," *American Journal of Legal History* 41 (1997): 440. James Rice considered the increasing role of lawyers in criminal trials in Maryland in "The Criminal Trial Before and After the Lawyers: Authority, Law, and Culture in Maryland Jury Trials, 1681–1837," *American Journal of Legal History* 40 (1996): 455, while Robert Ireland explored the ongoing significance of private prosecutions in "Privately Funded Prosecution of Crime in the Nineteenth-Century United States," *American Journal of Legal History* 39 (1995): 43.

Several other works provide significant glimpses of the nineteenth-century criminal trial in the course of a larger study. Jack Kenny Williams described felony trials in his study of crime in antebellum South Carolina, *Vogues in Villainy*; Allen Steinberg sketched the changes in Philadelphia's criminal justice system in *The Transformation of Criminal Justice*; and Laura Edwards examined trials and the legal process in North and South Carolina in *The People and Their Peace*. Less has been done on the rules of evidence and proof. Barbara Shapiro's study of Anglo-American rules of evidence, *Beyond "Reasonable Doubt" and "Probable Cause": Historical Perspectives on the Anglo-American Law of Evidence* (1991), is complemented by some studies of particular rules. See, for example, Alan G. Gless, "Self-Incrimination Privilege Development in the Nineteenth-Century Federal Courts: Questions of Procedure, Privilege, Production, Immunity and Compulsion," *American Journal of Legal History* 45 (2001): 391; G. S. Rowe, "Infanticide, Its Judicial Resolution, and Criminal Code Revision in Early Pennsylvania," *Proceedings of the American Philosophical Society* 135 (1991): 200; David McCord, "The English and American History of Voluntary Intoxication to Negate *Mens Rea*," *Journal of Legal History* [Great Britain], 11 (1990): 372; Jeffrey K. Sawyer, "'Benefit of Clergy' in Maryland and Virginia," *American Journal of Legal History* 34 (1990): 49 (tracing the doctrine's demise in the early nineteenth century). But aside from those works and a few specific case studies that treat evidentiary and procedural rules – see, for example, M. Clifford Harrison, "Murder in the Courtroom," *Virginia Calvacade* 17 (1967): 43 ("reasonable doubt" standard in relation to a 1912 murder trial) – more work could be done in this area. The only comprehensive study of the procedural and evidentiary shifts in criminal law is Michael Millender's unpublished dissertation, The Transformation of the American Criminal Trial, 1790–1875 (Ph.D. diss., Princeton University, 1996).

In contrast, the history of the insanity defense and its influence on the nineteenth-century criminal justice system has been the subject of a number of studies. They trace its rise (Alan Rodgers, "Murders and Madness: Law and Medicine in Nineteenth-Century Massachusetts," *Proceedings of the Massachusetts Historical Society* 106 [1994]: 53); the problems it caused (Charles E. Rosenberg, *The Trial of the Assassin Guiteau: Psychiatry and the Law in the Gilded Age* [1968]; Robert M. Ireland, "Insanity and the Unwritten Law," *American Journal of Legal History* 32 [1998]: 157); and efforts to reform it (Janet E. Tighe, "'Be It Ever So Little': Reforming the Insanity Defense in the Progressive Era," *Bulletin of the History of Medicine* 57 [1983]: 395).

Courts

There are a number of studies of specific criminal courts, most notably the juvenile justice system. Eric Schneider examined juvenile justice throughout the nineteenth century in his monograph *In the Web of Class: Delinquents and Reformers in Boston, 1810s–1930s* (1992). Other studies look at the rise of the distinctive juvenile court system at the end of the nineteenth century: David Tanenhaus, *Juvenile Justice in the Making* (2004); David Wolcott, "Juvenile Justice Before Juvenile Courts: Cops, Courts and Kids in Turn-of-the-Century Detroit," *Social Science History* 27 (2003): 109; Wolcott, "The Cop Will Get You." And a few studies have looked at misdemeanor and police courts. Steinberg's *Transformation of Criminal Law* describes the declining power of those petty courts in Philadelphia. His study ended in 1880, roughly the time when *Roots of Justice*, the study of felony and police courts in Alameda County, California, by Lawrence M. Friedman and Robert Perceival, picked up. Michael Willrich examined Progressive Era Chicago's experiment with a municipal court, intended to be a replacement for the corrupt police court system and a means of social control; see Willrich, *City of Courts: Socializing Progressive Era Chicago* (2003); see also Lynne M. Adrian and Joan E. Crowley, "Hoboes and Homeboys: The Demography of Misdemeanor Convictions in the Allegheny County Jail, 1892–1923," *Journal of Social History* 25 (1991): 345. But there is almost no work on post-trial matters like criminal appeals or pardons.

Likewise, more work could be devoted to other criminal justice systems. Of the few that have studied other systems, most deal with the criminal justice system for slaves and free blacks in the antebellum era: Campbell, 'The Victim of Prejudice and Hasty Consideration'; Morris, *Southern Slavery and the Law*; Seematter, "Trials and Confessions"; Schwartz, *Twice Condemned Slaves*; Henderson, "Spartan Slaves"; Flannigan, "Criminal Procedure in Slave Trials"; Edwards, "Slave Justice"; McPherson, ed., "Georgia Slave Trials, 1837–1841"; Coulter, "Four Slave Trials." For a study that explored the sort of process that was considered due to slaves, see Campbell, "The Victim of Prejudice and Hasty Consideration."

In contrast, very little work on the criminal justice systems applies to Native Americans in the nineteenth century (Brad Asher, *Beyond the Reservation: Indians, Settlers and Laws in the Washington Territory, 1853–1889* [1999]) or the processes by which those legal systems were created (Blue Clark, Lone Wolf v. Hitchcock: *Treaty Rights and Indian Law at the End of the Nineteenth Century* [1994]).

Plea Bargains

Trials were not, of course, the typical experience of defendants in twentieth-century criminal courts, where most cases were pleaded out. This practice had its beginnings in the nineteenth century. Summary jurisdiction, a practice that let magistrates try some minor criminal matters without a jury (or an indictment), offered one means of processing cases with little or no process. See, for example, Bruce Phillip Smith, "Circumventing the Jury: Petty Crime and Summary Jurisdiction in London and New York City, 1790–1855" (Ph.D. diss., Yale University, 1997). The development of plea bargaining allowed even felony cases to be resolved in summary fashion. See David J. Bodenhamer, "Criminal Sentencing in Antebellum America: A North–South Comparison," *Historical Social Research* [West Germany], 15 (1990): 77 (finding plea bargains in the North and South before the Civil War). And two studies have demonstrated the development's impact on conviction rates: Lane, *Violent Death in the City*; Monkkonen, *Murder in New York*. Another group of studies explores the relation between the rise of plea bargaining and the growth of State power: George Fisher, *Plea Bargaining's Triumph: A History of Plea Bargaining in America* (2004); Mary Vogel, "The Social Origins of Plea Bargaining: Conflict and Law in the Process of State Formation, 1830–1860," *Law and Society Review* 33 (1999): 161; Mike McCanville and Chester Mirsky, "The Rise of the Guilty Pleas: New York, 1800–1865," *Journal of Law and Society* 22 (1995): 443. Taking a contrary view, in another study I suggest that the rise of the plea bargain reflected frustrations with the unpredictable, ad hoc nature of criminal justice caused by the continued influence of popular forces on the courts; see Elizabeth Dale, *"People v. Coughlin* and the Criminal Jury in Late Nineteenth-Century Chicago," *Northern Illinois University Law Review* 28 (2008): 503.

Criminal Trials

Published criminal trial transcripts were popular literature in the nineteenth century. See Karen Halttunen, *Murder Most Foul* (1998); David Ray Papke, *Framing the Criminal: Crime, Cultural Work and the Loss of Critical Perspective, 1830–1990* (1987). An entire historical genre has arisen

around the study of individual criminal cases. Robert
Darnton called these works, which trace repercussions
of murders, scandals, riots, and catastrophes through the
social order, "incident studies"; see Darnton, "It Happened
One Night," *New York Review of Books* (June 24, 2004),
60. In an earlier essay, William Fisher called it "New
Historicism" after Stephen Greenblatt's work; see Fisher,
"Texts and Contexts: The Application to American Legal
History of the Methodologies of Intellectual History,"
Stanford Law Review 49 (1997): 1065.

Regardless of the name given to the genre, these studies illuminate the workings of the criminal justice system
in the long nineteenth century, tracing the ways in which
law intersected with social, moral, and political forces in
all sorts of trials. One of the articles Fisher cited as an
example of the approach was a misdemeanor trial – a
prosecution for keeping a pig in New York City: Hendrik
Hartog, "Pigs and Positivism," *Wisconsin Law Review*
(1985): 89. All sorts of crimes have been the subject of these
histories, including assassination (Charles E. Rosenbergh,
*The Trial of the Assassin Guiteau: Psychiatry and the
Law in the Gilded Age* [1968]), murder (e.g., Patricia
Cline Cohen, *The Murder of Helen Jewett*; Dale, *The
Rule of Justice*), manslaughter (Regina Morantz-Sanchez,
*Conduct Unbecoming a Woman: Medicine on Trial in
Turn-of-the-Century Brooklyn* [1999]), lynching (Mark
Curriden and Leroy Phillips, *Contempt of Court: The
Turn-of-the-Century Lynching That Launched a Hundred
Years of Federalism* [1999]), adultery (Richard Wightman
Fox, *Trials of Intimacy: Love and Loss in the Beecher–
Tilton Scandal* [1999]), aiding runaway slaves (Gary
Collinson, "'This Flagitious Offense': Daniel Webster and
the Shadrach Rescue Cases, 1851–1852," *New England
Quarterly* 68 [1995]: 609), and rebellion (Arthur Scherr,
"Governor James Monroe and the Southampton Slave

Resistance of 1799," *Historian* 61 [1999]: 557; Winthrop Jordan, *Tumult and Silence on Second Creek: An Inquiry into a Civil War Slave Conspiracy* [1993]).

Punishment

Imprisonment

The nineteenth century marked the shift from physical punishments (whipping, the stocks, executions) to the incarceration of prisoners in penitentiaries, and a number of books and articles focus on that shift and its causes. Rebecca McLennan offers an overview of the politics of imprisonment in *The Crisis of Imprisonment: Protest, Politics and the Development of the American Penal State* (2008), though her study focuses on New York. The start of the penitentiary movement at the beginning of the nineteenth century is described in other monographs, notably Adam J. Hirsch, *The Rise of the Penitentiary: Prison and Punishment in Early America* (1992), and Michael Meranze, *Laboratories of Virtue: Punishment, Revolution and Authority in Philadelphia, 1760–1835* (1996). Shifts in theories of imprisonment are discussed in McLennan, *Crisis of Imprisonment*, and in Stephen Garton, "Criminal Propensities: Psychiatry, Classifications, and Imprisonment in New York State, 1916–1940," *Social History of Medicine* 23 (2010): 79.

For most of the nineteenth century, penitentiaries were a northern phenomenon; southern states resisted it through the antebellum era (Ayers, *Vengeance and Justice*; Williams, *Vogues in Villainy*) and turned to convict labor during Reconstruction. See Karin Shapiro, *A New South Rebellion: The Battle Against Convict Labor in the Tennessee Coalfields, 1871–1896* (1998); Gavin Wright, "Convict Labor After Emancipation: Old South or New South?" *Georgia Historical Quarterly* 81 (1997): 452; Alex Lichtenstein, "Good Roads and Chain Gangs

in the Progressive South: 'The Negro Convict as a Slave,'"
Journal of Southern History 59 (1993): 85.

It was not until the end of the century that southern states finally embraced the penitentiary (Matthew J.
Mancini, *One Dies, Get Another: Convict Leasing in the
American South, 1866–1928* [1996]). By that point some
northern states had begun to experiment with reformatories. See Paul Keve, "Building a Better Prison: The First
Three Decades of the Detroit House of Corrections,"
Michigan Historical Review 25 (1999): 1; Mark Colvin,
*Penitentiaries, Reformatories, and Chain Gangs: Social
Theory and the History of Punishment in Nineteenth-
Century America* (1997); Alexander W. Pisciotta,
*Benevolent Repression: Social Control and the American
Reformatory Movement* (1994); Robert G. Waite, "From
Penitentiary to Reformatory: Alexander Maconochie
Walter Crofton, Zebulon Brockway, and the Road to Prison
Reform: New South Wales, Ireland, and Elmire, New York,
1840–1870," *Criminal Justice History* 12 (1991): 85.

As that collection of works suggests, this is another area
where the literature emphasizes regional difference. See
David J. Bodenhamer, "Criminal Sentencing in Antebellum
America: A North–South Comparison," *Historical Social
Research* [West Germany], 15 (1990): 77. Much of the
work, however, focuses on imprisonment in individual
states or regions: Theresa Jach, "Reform versus Reality in
the Progressive Era Texas Prison," *Journal of the Gilded
Age and Progressive Era* 41 (2005): 53; Keith Edgerton,
Montana Justice: Power, Punishment, and the Penitentiary
(2004); Jeffrey Koeher and Walter L. Brieschke, "Menard:
Development of a Nineteenth-Century Prison," *Journal
of the Illinois State Historical Society* 96 (2003): 230;
Jayce McKay, "Reforming Prisoners and Prisons: Iowa's
State Prisons – Their First Hundred Years," *Annals of
Iowa* 60 (2001): 139; Vivien M. L. Miller, "Reinventing

the Penitentiary: Punishment in Florida, 1868–1923," *American Nineteenth Century History* [Great Britain] 1 (2000): 82; Larry Goldsmith, "'To Profit by His Skill and to Traffic in His Crime': Prison Labor in Early 19th-Century Massachusetts," *Labor History* [Great Britain], 40 (1999): 439; Timothy Dodge, "Hard Labor at the New Hampshire State Prison," *Historical New Hampshire* 47 (1992): 113; Gary Kremer, "Politics, Punishment and Profit: Convict Labor in the Missouri State Penitentiary, 1875–1900," *Gateway Heritage* 13 (1992): 28; Martha Myers and James Massey, "Race, Labor, and Punishment in Postbellum Georgia," *Social Problems* 38 (1991): 267; Donald Walker, *Penology for Profit: A History of the Texas Prison System, 1867–1912* (1988); Paul Knepper, "Converting Idle Labor into Substantial Wealth: Arizona's Convict Lease System," *Journal of Arizona History* 31 (1990): 79; Glen Gildermeister, *Prison Labor and Convict Competition with Free Workers in Industrializing America, 1840–1890* (1987). Yet a glance at the literature suggests that the profit motive cut across state borders. See McLennan, *The Crime of Punishment*; William Staples, "In the Interests of the State: Production Politics in the Nineteenth-Century Prison," *Sociological Perspectives* 33 (1990): 375. This suggests that more work could be done to test the comparative assumptions, to examine whether and when trends in imprisonment crossed regions and state boundaries.

There are other possibilities for comparative study. Some works have made international comparisons. For example, in *Harsh Justice: Criminal Punishment and the Widening Divide between America and Europe* (2003), James Whitman explored the way punishment regimes in the United States and European nations have diverged over the past three hundred years. A number of other studies have focused on intranational comparisons.

In an article written in 1985, Nicole Hahn Rafter urged that more work be done to learn about women prisoners; see Rafter, "Gender, Prisons and Prison History," *Social Science History* 9 (1985): 233. Before she wrote, there had been only a handful of articles examining the experiences of women in prison: Robert Waite, "Necessary to Isolate the Female Prisoners: Women Convicts and the Women's Ward at the Old Idaho Penitentiary," *Iowa Yesterdays* 29 (1985): 2; W. David Lewis, "The Female Criminal and the Prisons of New York, 1825–1845," *New York History* 42 (1961): 215. Since then, a number of studies have explored the special experiences of women prisoners; Mara Dodge has written several articles on this subject, including "'The Most Degraded of Their Sex, If Not of Humanity': Female Prisoners at the Illinois State Penitentiary at Joliet, 1859–1900," *Journal of Illinois History* 2 (1999): 205, and "'One Female Prisoner Is of More Trouble Than Twenty Males': Women Convicts in Illinois Prisons, 1835–1896," *Journal of Social History* 32 (1999): 907. Other historians have followed suit: Leslie Patrick, "Ann Hinson: A Little-Known Woman in the Country's Premier Prison, Eastern State Penitentiary, 1831," *Pennsylvania History* 67 (2000): 361; Joan Jensen, "Sexuality on a Northern Frontier: The Gendering and Disciplining of Rural Wisconsin Women, 1850–1920," *Agricultural History* 73 (1999): 136; Nan Wolverton, "Bottomed Out: Female Chair Seaters in Nineteenth-Century New England," *Dublin Seminar for New England Folklife* 23 (1998): 175; Anne M. Butler, "Still in Chains: Black Women in Western Prisons, 1865–1910," *Western Historical Quarterly* 20 (1989): 18. These works invite comparisons, either of the ways in which male and female prisoners were treated or of the different ways that women experienced imprisonment.

The articles by Patrick and Butler, which deal with the situation of black women, are complemented by other works that examine the intersection of race, prison, and punishment in the nineteenth century. Again, many of these studies are local; see, for example, Mary Ellen Curren, *Black Prisoners and Their World, Alabama, 1865–1900* (2000); Lynne M. Adrian and Joan E. Crowley, "Hoboes and Homeboys: The Demography of Misdemeanor Convictions in the Allegheny County Jail, 1892–1923," *Journal of Social History* 25 (1991): 345; Michael S. Hindus, "Black Justice under White Law: Criminal Prosecutions of Blacks in Antebellum South Carolina," *Journal of American History* 63 (1976): 575. Some are regional: Mancini, *One Dies, Get Another*; McKanna, *Homicide, Race, and Justice in the American West, 1880–1920*. Still others are comparative, for example, Henry Douglas Kammerling, "'Too Much Time for the Crime I Done': Race, Ethnicity, and the Politics of Punishment in Illinois and South Carolina, 1865 to 1900" (Ph.D. diss., University of Illinois, 1999). There are also studies that examine how ethnicity influenced punishment: Brad Asher, "'Their Own Domestic Difficulties': Intra-Indian Crime and White Law in Western Washington Territory, 1873–1889," *Western Historical Quarterly* 27 (1996): 189; Linda S. Parker, "Statutory Changes and Ethnicity in Sex Crimes in Four California Counties, 1880–1920," *Western Legal History* 6 (1993): 69; David Beesley, "More Than *People v. Hall*: Chinese Immigrants and American Law in Sierra Nevada County, 1850–1920," *Locus* 3 (1991): 123. Once again, the body of literature invites serious study of whether, and how, imprisonment was applied to members of different groups.

More could also be done regarding the imprisonment of minors. Some studies trace the treatment of young convicts back to the beginning of the nineteenth century; see, for example, Gary Shockley, "A History of the Incarceration of Juveniles in Tennessee, 1796–1970," *Tennessee Historical Quarterly* 43 (1984): 229; Christopher Span,

"Educational and Social Responses to African American Juvenile Delinquents in Nineteenth-Century New York and Philadelphia," *Journal of Negro Education* 71 (2002): 108; Eric Schneider, *In the Web of Class: Delinquents and Reformers in Boston, 1810s–1930s* (1992). Other studies look at the punishment of juveniles at the end of the nineteenth century: David Tanenhaus, *Juvenile Justice in the Making* (2004), David Wolcott, "Juvenile Justice Before Juvenile Courts: Cops, Courts and Kids in Turn-of-the-Century Detroit," *Social Science History* 27 (2003): 109; Wolcott, "'The Cop Will Get You'; Randall G. Shelden, "A History of the Shelby County Industrial and Training School," *Tennessee Historical Quarterly* 51 (1991): 96; Mary R. Block, "Child-Saving Laws of Louisville and Jefferson County, 1854–1894: A Socio-Legal History," *Filson Club History Quarterly* 66 (1992): 232.

Other articles specifically examine girls imprisoned in the juvenile justice system: Sharon E. Wood, "Savage Girls: The 1899 Riot at the Mitchellville Girls School," *Iowa Heritage Illustrated* 80 (1999): 108; Georgina Hickey, "Rescuing the Working Girl: Agency and Conflict in the Michigan Reform School for Girls, 1879–1893," *Michigan Historical Review* 20 (1994): 1. Once again, this wealth of material points to a need for comparative studies of these different groups. In addition, more work might be done to consider the role of class in the process of imprisonment. Progressive Era reformers, like John Peter Altgeld of Illinois, worried about the age, class, and gender of prisoners in their attacks on the criminal justice system; see Altgeld, *Our Penal Machinery and Its Victims* (1884). Some studies have matched their focus; see, for example, Georgina Hickey, "Rescuing the Working Girl: Agency and Conflict in the Michigan Reform School for Girls, 1979–1893," *Michigan Historical Review* 20 (1994): 1. But there is room for additional work.

Other Forms of Punishment

Of course, not all defendants convicted of crimes were imprisoned. Some were executed. The major study of capital punishment in the nineteenth-century United States is Louis Masur, *Rites of Execution: Capital Punishment and the Transformation of American Culture, 1776–1865* (1991), but other studies have looked at capital punishment in particular states: Philip B. Mackey, *Hanging in the Balance: Anti-Capital Punishment Movement in New York State, 1776–1861* (1982); Negley Teeters, *Scaffold and Chair: A Compilation of Their Use in Pennsylvania, 1682–1962* (1963).

Those convicted of crimes could be punished in other ways as well. Until the 1840s, white men found guilty of bastardy in South Carolina might be sold into servitude to pay for their child's upkeep (Richard B. Morris, *Government and Labor in Early America* [1942]), and whites from that state who were convicted of other crimes could be whipped until that punishment was limited to blacks in the 1840s (Williams, *Vogues in Villiany*). California relied on whipping as punishment until the end of the Civil War (Gordon Bakken Morris, "The Courts, the Legal Profession, and the Development of Law in Early California," *California History*, 81 [2003]: 74), and Virginia did so through the end of Reconstruction (William A. Blair, "Justice versus Law and Order: The Battles over the Reconstruction of Virginia's Minor Judiciary, 1865–1870," *Virginia Magazine of History and Biography* 103 [1995]: 157). Kentucky required whipping for many petty crimes until the end of the nineteenth century (Robert M. Ireland, "The Debate over Whipping Criminals in Kentucky," *Register of the Kentucky Historical Society* 100 [2002]: 5). The literature suggests there was a racial dimension to the punishment chosen, but more could be done to explore this issue.

Pardons

The pardon power is dealt with in general studies of crim-
inal justice. In addition, some studies deal with pardons:
Vivian Miller, *Crime, Sexual Violence and Clemency:
Florida's Pardon Board and Penal System in the Progressive
Era* (2000); Barry Salkin, "The Pardoning Power in
Antebellum Pennsylvania," *Pennsylvania Magazine of
History and Biography* 100 (1976): 507.

Punishment of the Insane

In his study David Rothman considered insane asylums as
well as prisons, and other scholars have pursued a similar course, particularly emphasizing the degree to which
both types of institution were viewed as a necessary means
of social control. See, for example, Marvin E. Schultz,
"'Running the Risks of Experiments': The Politics of Penal
Reform in Tennessee, 1807–1829," *Tennessee Historical
Quarterly* 52 (1993): 86. The connections between the institutions go far deeper; in many states for much of the antebellum era, those judged insane for any reason were housed in
jails. See Frank Narbury, "Dorothy Dix and the Founding
of Illinois' First Mental Institution," *Journal of the Illinois
State Historical Society* 92 (1999): 13. Reformers, notably Dorothy Dix, began to challenge that in the 1840s and
1850s, and by the start of the Civil War there were special
asylums for the insane in a number of eastern states, as far
west as Illinois and even in southern states like Alabama. See
Bill L. Weaver, "Establishing and Organizing the Alabama
Insane Hospital, 1846–1861," *Alabama Review* 48 (1995):
219. More states followed in the period after the Civil War.
See, for example, William D. Erickson, "'Something Must
Be Done for Them': Establishment of Minnesota's First
Hospital for the Insane," *Minnesota History* 53 (1992): 42;
Russell Hollander, "Life at the Washington Asylum for the
Insane, 1871–1880," *Historian* 44 (1982): 229. Studies of

the creation of these institutions provide a means of tracing shifts in understandings of punishment, incarceration, and rehabilitation, a point suggested by some works, for example, Andrew T. Scull, "Madness and Segregative Control: The Rise of the Insane Asylum," *Social Problems* 24 (1977): 337; Schultz, "Running the Risks of Experiments"; Ellen Dwyer, *Homes for the Mad: Life Inside Two Nineteenth-Century Asylums* (1987) (comparing Utica, founded in 1843, and Willard, founded in 1863). However, more could be done to engage these relations and explore their consequences.

Cultural Influence

One question in the literature on homicide is whether particular cultural forces led to the high rates of homicide and low rates of punishment in the United States. See the forum on homicide in *American Historical Review*, 111 (2006): 75. Studies of punishment explore a variation on this issue: why some crimes of violence were punished and some were not. Many follow Wyatt-Brown, *Southern Honor*, attributing responses to violence in both the North and South to honor culture. See, for example, Lane, *Homicide in America* (noting the existence of plebian honor culture among the working class in the North). But others ascribe failures to punish violence to other forces. William Lynwood Montell, for example, argued that the lawless violence he traced in late-nineteenth-century Kentucky had its roots in a combination of a whiskey-driven culture, the heritage of guerrilla fighting during and after the Civil War, and an intense localism caused by an underdeveloped economy; see Montell, *Killings: Folk Justice in the Upper South* (1986). Fitzhugh Brundage found that economic differences gave rise to the different lynching rates in Georgia and Virginia between 1880 and 1930, and that changes in economic circumstances helped reformers bring lynching to an end; see Brundage, *Lynching in the New South*.

Wyatt-Brown's analysis in *Southern Honor* raises a number of issues that we would now consider problems of gender. More recent studies address that issue more explicitly, suggesting the different ways that gender norms dictated reactions to crimes: Guy Reed, "The Wicked World: Masculinities and Portrayals of Sex, Crime and Sports in the National Police Gazette," *American Journalism* 22 (2005): 61; Susan Sessions Rugh, "Civilizing the Countryside: Class, Gender and Crime in Nineteenth-Century Rural Illinois," *Agricultural History* 76 (2002): 58; Hendrik Hartog, "Lawyering, Husband's Rights, and 'the Unwritten Law' in Nineteenth-Century America," *Journal of American History* 84 (1997): 67; Vivian Miller, "Wife Killers and Evil Temptresses: Gender, Pardons and Respectability in Florida, 1889–1914," *Florida Historical Quarterly* 75 (1996): 44; Martha Merrill Umphrey, "The Dialogics of Legal Meaning: Spectacular Trials, the Unwritten Law, and Narratives of Criminal Responsibility," *Law and Society Review* 33 (1999): 393; Gordon M. Bakken, "The Limits of Patriarchy: Women's Rights and 'Unwritten Law' in the West," *Historian* 60 (1998): 702.

Extralegal Justice

As the work on cultural influences on law suggests, the formal workings of criminal law in the nineteenth century were shaped by popular forces that functioned outside the courts and often outside the law, but only a few works explore this area of criminal law. Studies of popular justice have typically emphasized its extralegal and violent aspects, looking particularly at duels, vigilante groups, and lynching. A number of major books in this area – Wyatt-Brown, *Southern Honor*; McGrath, *Gunfighters,*

Highwaymen, and Vigilantes; W. Fitzhugh Brundage, *Lynching in the New South: Georgia and Virginia, 1880–1930* (1993); Richard Maxwell Brown, *Strains of Violence: Historical Studies of American Violence and Vigilantism* (1975) – have been complemented by recent articles that consider lynching and vigilante activity in particular times and places. For articles on vigilantes, see Cindy Higgins, "Frontier Protection and Social Network: The Anti-Horse Thief Association in Kansas," *Journal of the West* 42 (2003): 63; Karlos K. Hill, "Black Vigilantism: The Rise and Decline of African American Lynch Mob Activity in the Mississippi and Arkansas Deltas, 1883–1923," *Journal of African American History* 95 (2010): 26; Paul Musgrave, "A Primitive Method of Enforcing the Law," *Indiana Magazine of History* 102 (2006): 187; Michael J. Pfeifer, "Law, Society and Violence in the Antebellum Midwest: The 1857 Eastern Iowa Vigilante Movement," *Annals of Iowa* 64 (2005): 139. For recent articles and books on lynching, see Paul R. Spitzzeri, "Judge Lynch in Session: Popular Justice in Los Angeles, 1850–1870," *Southern California Quarterly* 87 (2005): 83; Pfeifer, *Rough Justice*.

A number of studies deal with duels. See, for example, Wyatt-Brown, *Southern Honor*; Jack Kenny Williams, *Dueling in the Old South* (2000). I discuss dueling as an expression of popular sovereignty in "Popular Sovereignty: A Case Study from the Antebellum Era," *Constitutional Mythologies: New Perspectives on Controlling the State* (2011). There are any number of studies of specific duels; for a sampling see Lee Ann Caldwell, "An Averted Duel, Augusta, 1843," *Georgia Historical Quarterly* 65 (1981): 323; James M. Denham, "The Reed–Alston Duel and Politics in Territorial Florida," *Florida Historical Quarterly* 68 (1990): 427; Donald Gill, "The Dueling Doctors of Stockton," *Pacific History* 25 (1981): 52.

Mobs have been a subject of much study, although many of the histories of mobs and mobbing have not considered them as examples of extralegal judgment or punishment. The English background of the mob is sketched in E. P. Thompson, "The Moral Economy of the Crowd," *Past and Present* 50 (1971): 76. The mob's Americanization is described in Pauline Maier, "Popular Uprisings and Civil Authority in Eighteenth-Century America," *William and Mary Quarterly* 27 (1970): 3; Barbara Clark Smith, "Food Riots and the American Revolution," *William and Mary Quarterly* 51 (1994): 3. For studies that look generally at the place of mobs in U.S. history, see David Grimsted, "Rioting in Its Jacksonian Setting," *American Historical Review* 77 (1972): 361; Carl E. Prince, "The Great 'Riot Year': Jacksonian Democracy and Patterns of Violence in 1824," *Journal of the Early Republic* 5 (1985): 1. Examples of studies of specific riots include Michael Feldberg, *The Philadelphia Riots of 1844* (1975); Peter Haebler, "Nativism, Liquor and Riots," *Historical New Hampshire* 46 (1984): 122; Theresa A. Harrison, "George Thompson and the 1851 'Anti-Abolitionist Riot," *Historical Journal of Western Massachusetts* 5 (1976): 36; Linda Kerber, "Abolitionists and Amalgamators: The New York City Race Riots of 1834," *New York History* 48 (1964): 28; Paul O. Weinbaum, "Temperance, Politics and the New York City Riots of 1857," *New York Historical Quarterly* (1975): 246.

Another area of extralegal justice that has been the subject of extensive analysis is the "unwritten law." In addition to the articles already referred to – Hartog, "Lawyering, Husband's Rights, and 'the Unwritten Law'"; Umphrey, "The Dialogics of Legal Meaning"; Bakken, "The Limits of Patriarchy" – a number of studies consider the unwritten law in particular contexts: Rosemary Gartner and Jim Phillips, "The Creefield–Mitchell Case, Seattle 1906:

The Unwritten Law in the Pacific Northwest," *Pacific Northwest Quarterly* 94 (2003): 69; Robert Ireland, "The Thompson–Davis Case and the Unwritten Law," *Filson Club Historical Quarterly* 62 (1888): 417; Robert Ireland, "Death to the Libertine: The McFarland–Richardson Case Revisited," *New York History* 68 (1987): 191. Robert Ireland has written several articles that engage the unwritten law more generally; see, for example, Ireland, "Insanity and the Unwritten Law," *American Journal of Legal History* 32 (1988): 157; Ireland, "Frenzied and Fallen Females: Women and Sexual Dishonor in the Nineteenth Century United States," *Journal of Women's History* 4 (1992): 95.

But extralegal justice was not only violent. Gossip networks could be used to judge misconduct and punish elite wrongdoers, as Peggy Eaton and Andrew Jackson learned to their chagrin in the 1820s. See John F. Marszalek, *The Petticoat Affair: Manners, Mutiny, and Sex in Andrew Jackson's White House* (1997). Workers used shaming and shunning punishments against strike breakers in antebellum Philadelphia and late-nineteenth-century Tampa. See Feldberg, *Philadelphia Riots*; Nancy Hewitt, *Southern Discomfort: Women's Actions in Tampa, Florida, 1880s – 1920s* (2001). Extralegal activities could also be an expression of resistance. See George Graham Perry III, "A Bend in the River: An Investigation of Black Agency, Autonomy, and Resistance in Memphis Tennessee (1846–1866)," *Western Tennessee Historical Society* 62 (2008): 44. Furthermore, church groups disciplined those who violated congregational norms. See generally Edwards, *People and Their Peace*; Elizabeth Dale, "A Different Sort of Justice: The Informal Courts of Public Opinion in Antebellum South Carolina," *South Carolina Law Review* 54 (2003): 627; Christopher Waldrep, "'So Much Sin': The Decline of Religious Discipline and the 'Tidal Wave' of Crime,'" *Journal of Social History* 25 (1990): 535; Henry Stroupe,

"'Cite Them Both to Attend the Next Church Conference':
Social Control by North Carolina Baptist Churches,"
North Carolina Historical Review 52 (1975): 156.

But for all that, we can go further. As I suggested earlier,
more could be done to explore when and how these different activities served to judge and punish others. We also
need to consider the different ways that extralegal justice
related to the State. There were instances when nineteenth-
century popular justice mirrored the State, punishing acts
that the formal law recognized was wrong. There were
also moments when popular justice went beyond the scope
of law, punishing those who committed acts the formal
rules did not define as criminal. Historians of crime and
criminal law need to do more to consider when violence,
shaming, or shunning are expressions of popular justice
and what they tell us about justice and informal processes
of law. And we can also do more to consider when the
popular will was expressed. The obvious place to start is
with the jury system. Why and how often did grand juries
take matters into their own hands? What about petty
juries? Studies suggest that jury nullification had come to
an end with the rise of judicial review before the Civil War;
see, for example, Nelson, *The Americanization of the
Common Law*, Kramer, *The People Themselves*; Clay S.
Conrad, *Jury Nullification: The Evolution of a Doctrine*
(1998). But jury nullification was not formally outlawed
on the federal level until the decision in *Sparf and Hansen
v. United States* (1895), remained a right in Illinois until
People v. Bruner (1931), and continues to be a constitutional right to this day in Maryland. Several articles
examine jury nullification: Dale, "Popular Sovereignty":
Matthew Harrington, "The Law-Finding Function of
the American Jury," *Wisconsin Law Review* (1999): 337;
David J. Bodenhamer, "The Democratic Impulse and Legal
Change in the Age of Jackson: The Example of Criminal

Juries in Antebellum Indiana," *The Historian* 54 (1983): 206. More could be done to explore its extent in the nineteenth century and to test its influence.

How else did the people influence the courts? Did the end of private prosecutions mark the point at which private influence no longer determined who could be prosecuted and for what? Or were there other ways that individuals or groups could influence what crimes would be prosecuted and who would be tried? There were any number of roles private people could play even at the earliest stages of the criminal justice process: as police officers (Edwards, *People and Their Peace*), as bounty hunters (Stuart H. Traub, "Rewards, Bounty Hunting, and Criminal Justice in the West, 1865–1900," *Western Historical Quarterly* 19 [1988]: 287 [tracing the way that bounty was used to involve private citizens in the criminal process]), or as participants in raids by citizens' leagues such as the preventive societies of New York (Gilfoyle, *City of Eros* [the formation of preventive societies opposed to vice, 1865–1880]). How did those popular forces interact with the formal processes of law, and when or why did they supplant them? See generally Craig B. Little and Christopher P. Sheffield, "Frontiers and Criminal Justice: English Private Prosecution Societies and American Vigilantism, in the Eighteenth and Nineteenth Centuries," *American Sociological Review* 48 (1983): 796 (arguing that English extralegal processes were appendages of criminal justice, while American extralegal activities were often alternatives to formal law). Finally, since all of these processes seem to be part of the larger whole, we need to develop some theoretical perspectives from which to compare these extralegal forces. An article by Benoît Garnot provides a typology of popular justice that could serve as a starting point; see Garnot, "Justice, infrajustice, parajustice et extrajustice dans la France d'Ancien Régime," *Crime, Histoire & Sociétés* 4 (2000): 103.

Studies of Federal Criminal Justice

A symposium in the *Law & History Review* 4 (1986): 223 addresses the issue of federal criminal law, considering its constitutionality and the specific issue of a federal common law of crimes. The question of a federal common law of crimes is also addressed in the context of the *Hudson and Goodwin* case in Gary D. Rowe, "Note: Sound of Silence: *United States v. Hudson and Goodwin*: The Jeffersonian Ascendency and the Abolition of Federal Common Law Crimes," *Yale Law Journal* 101 (1991): 919.

There are several studies of the writ of habeas corpus. William Wiecek put the Habeas Corpus Act of 1867 in historical context in his study "The Great Writ and Reconstruction: The Habeas Corpus Act of 1867," *Journal of Southern History* 36 (1970): 530–548. Some recent studies consider habeas corpus from a constitutional perspective. The first, a dissertation by Justin J. Wert, "Habeas Corpus and the Politics of Individual Rights" (University of Pennsylvania, 2005), considered it from a rights-based perspective. Cary Howard Federman's book, *The Body and the State: Habeas Corpus and American Jurisprudence* (Albany, 2006), which was based on his dissertation, "The Primacy of Right and the Procedures of Federalism: The Development of Habeas Corpus and Federal–State Relations, 1789–1991" (University of Virginia, 1996), looks at the manner in which habeas corpus law tried to balance the interests of federalism and rights-based claims. Habeas corpus was of particular importance during the Civil War and Reconstruction, and in addition to Weicek's article several other studies explore the writ in those periods. See, for example, Lawrence H. Larsen, "Draft Riot in Wisconsin, 1862," *Civil War History* 7 (1961): 421–427; David Everitt, "1871 War on Terror," *American History* 38 (2003): 26–33; Richard

Zuczek, "The Federal Government's Attack on the Ku Klux Klan: A Reassessment," *South Carolina Historical Magazine*, 97 (1996): 47–64. See also Frank J. Williams, "Civil Liberties v. National Security: The Long Shadow of the Civil War," *Civil War* Times 46 (2007): 24–29 (a comparative study exploring the suspension of habeas corpus during the Civil War and the federal government's response to terrorism after September 11). In addition, the issue of habeas corpus claims comes up in the context of federal prosecution of illegal immigrants, particularly the case of the Chinese taken into custody after the Chinese Exclusion Act of 1882. See Christian Fritz, "A Nineteenth Century 'Habeas Corpus Mill': The Chinese before the Federal Courts in California," *American Journal of Legal History* 32 (1988): 347–372.

There are also studies of particular federal crimes: Kathleen J. Frydl, "Kidnapping and State Development in the United States," *Studies in American Political Development* 20 (2006): 18; Foster, *Moral Reconstruction*; Keire, "The Vice Trust"; Hamm, *Shaping the Eighteenth Amendment: Temperance Reform, Legal Culture, and the Polity.*

Crime and Popular Culture

In the nineteenth century, crime and criminal trials were a part of everyday life. Trial reports from criminal cases were published throughout the country, and a number of those books are available online in the Study in Scarlet Collection at the Harvard Law School Library. For cultural histories based on these accounts, see Daniel Cohen, *Pillars of Salt, Monuments of Grace: New England Crime Literature and the Origins of American Popular Culture, 1674–1860* (1993); Karen Halttunen, *Murder Most Foul* (1998). Weeklies, most notably the *Police Gazette*, also offered accounts of trials from around the country. And beginning in the mid-nineteenth century, newspapers increasingly reported on sensational trials as well, a process described from a regional perspective in Michael Trotti, *The Body in the Reservoir: Murder and Sensationalism in the South* (2008); Andie Tucher, *Froth and Scum: Truth, Beauty, Goodness, and the Axe Murder in America's First Mass Medium* (1994); David Ray Papke, *Framing the Criminal: Crime, Cultural Work, and the Loss of Critical Perspective, 1830–1900* (1987).

INDEX